Advance praise...

'Martin Clark is an inspiring, effective and purposeful guide to this emerging field. He shows that you and I have a role to play in the revolution taking place. Everyone can become more socially entrepreneurial.'

Lord Hastings of Scarisbrick, CBE, global head of citizenship and diversity, KPMG

'This book captures the excitement, passion and potential of social enterprises, and the social entrepreneurs behind them. I wholeheartedly recommend it as the essential first step to understanding what's happening and how to be a part of it.'

Walter Herriot, OBE, managing director, St John's Innovation Centre, Cambridge

'If you want to join the movement for lasting social impact, this book is for you. Whether you are in business, charity or just want to make some corner of our world a better place, you'll find within these covers a fund of inspiring case studies, thorough analysis and practical tools to help you.'

Ram Gidoomal, CBE, professor of entrepreneurship, Middlesex University

D1124283

By buying this book you are helping to support the work of the charity Citylife, which will receive a quarter of the royalties on sales. Citylife offers charities and communities a mechanism, the charitable bond, to generate funding for the issues they care about. It also provides affordable space to enable social enterprises to fulfil their potential.

www.citylifeltd.org

The Social
Entrepreneur
Revolution

**Doing good by making money,
making money by doing good**

MARTIN CLARK

Copyright © 2009 Martin Clark

First published in 2009 by:

Marshall Cavendish Limited
Fifth Floor
32–38 Saffron Hill
London EC1N 8FH
United Kingdom
T: +44 (0)20 7421 8120
F: +44 (0)20 7421 8121
sales@marshallcavendish.co.uk
www.marshallcavendish.co.uk

The right of Martin Clark to be identified as the author of this work has been asserted by him in accordance with the Copyright, Designs and Patents Act 1988.

A CIP record for this book is available from the British Library

ISBN 978-1-905736-42-3

Designed and typeset by Phoenix Photosetting,
Lordswood, Chatham, Kent

Printed and bound in Great Britain by
MPG Books Ltd, Bodmin, Cornwall

To Bekki, Molly and Grace
for their inspiration and love

Contents

Acknowledgements

I could not have completed this book without the help and inspiration of the following people.

The social entrepreneurs featured in this book are the reason why it was written – their courage, skill and determination are amazing. Special thanks to those who took time out of their busy lives to respond to my questions: Somsook Boonyabancha, Colin Crooks, Eugenie Harvey, Reed Paget, Norma Redfearn, Jack Sim, Jeff Skoll and Sue Welland.

Craig Dearden-Phillips was a constant encouragement, and read a draft in the middle of the night despite producing his own book on a related subject. A true social entrepreneur and inspiration. I had other invaluable comments on the manuscript from Mike Sewell of Cambridge Publishers, Gavin Howard and Bekki Clark (my fiercest and friendliest critic). The social entrepreneur self-assessment was improved by comments from Oliver Clark, Suzanne Goff, Gavin Howard and Tim and Celia Phipps. Thanks also to Mike Southon and Chris West for permission to use their 'Beermat Entrepreneur' brand in Chapter 8.

I am grateful to the board and staff of Citylife (poor Tim and Christine have borne the brunt of my moods) for the sabbatical during which I started the thinking and writing; and to David McDowall and Elizabeth Laird for the inspirational location of their flat in Edinburgh where the first hesitant words were written.

At Cyan Books, I will always be grateful to Martin Liu for taking a chance with the idea and a new author, and for his early shaping; to Pom Somkabcharti for her patience and enthusiasm; and to Jill Willder for her incisive editing. At the earliest stage, Keith Sands gave me valuable advice to capture the concept and communicate it.

And above all, I thank Bekki, Molly and Grace for the sacrifice they made. I cannot hope to repay them, but I hope they will consider it worthwhile if anyone reads, benefits from and acts on this book.

1

Introduction

'Soon all entrepreneurs will be social entrepreneurs.'
Pamela Hartigan, managing director,
Schwab Foundation

Half a world away. A generation apart. Different culture, different skin. Two men who could hardly be more different: one a young British TV star, the other a senior banker from South Asia. Yet they are united by one vision: self-sufficient people who can feed themselves without charity.

As Jamie Oliver was born in the mid-1970s, a young economics professor called Muhammad Yunus was experiencing a life-changing event that led to one of the greatest innovations in tackling world poverty. Eight years later, as Yunus launched his world-changing new organisation, the young Jamie Oliver had just started working in his father's pub restaurant. As an adult, he went on to set up his own chain of restaurants to change people's lives. The price of a main course in one of those restaurants now is what it cost to start Yunus's revolution 30 years earlier.

Yunus, now in his 60s, has helped over 5 million people feed their own families by inventing a new financial system which is spreading across the globe and for which he won a Nobel Prize. Oliver, still in his 30s, found a way to feed 3 million schoolchildren better every day and is regarded as a national treasure. The thing that unites them is that celebrity chef Jamie Oliver and banker to the poor Muhammad Yunus are both social entrepreneurs.

Change is coming from unexpected directions. We live in very interesting times.

Businesses are urgently looking for sustainable and socially responsible ways to operate. Government wants more public services to be delivered economically at a community level. Wealthy business people are looking for more creative ways to be philanthropic. Consumers are increasingly concerned with ethical, social and environmental issues in their purchasing decisions. And charities want to know how to move away from dependence on grant funding.

All these trends are taking the worlds of business, public sector and personal lifestyle into uncharted territory, opening up all sorts of opportunities for new partnerships and innovations. Who will be the winners in this new world? Will it be the big business of the twentieth century, reshaped for more discerning twenty-first century consumers? Will the public sector somehow reinvent itself? Will the traditional voluntary or charitable sector step into the breach?

No, it will be the social entrepreneurs. People like Jamie Oliver and Muhammad Yunus. And unlike them too. An explosion of activity in every continent that is already creating a better world and contains within it a vision that can inspire – and involve – us all.

Social entrepreneurs are perfectly adapted to prosper in a climate of change and uncertainty. They thrive on a subtle blend (as Jamie might say) of business and charity, ethics and enthusiasm, reliability and innovation. And a sense of humour.

But is it possible to be businesslike and charitable at the same time? Ethical without being dull? Entrepreneurial without being ruthless? And having a sense of humour while also being deadly serious about the mission?

Social entrepreneurs all over the world are already rewriting the recipe book, mixing social impact and profit. We shall look at many different examples as the book unfolds. But much more needs to be done to realise the full potential of this new approach. Social entrepreneurship has the power to transform corporate practice and its public image; revitalise public service delivery; and sharpen up the charitable sector.

So who are these strange creatures, social entrepreneurs? They are an intriguing mixture of business people with a strong social conscience; charity managers who want to build sustainable and customer-focused organisations; and public servants who are brave enough to admit that new approaches are required to improve the services we all need. In short, they are people who have realised it is possible to do good by making money, and make money by doing good.

Despite the rapid growth in social entrepreneurship over the past 10 years, it is still a well-kept secret as far as the general public is concerned. This book is an attempt to raise awareness about the sector in general. It is for entrepreneurs who are interested in the business opportunities that the social dimension brings, innovators in the public and charitable sectors who are serious about driving change, young people who will increasingly be studying the methods of social entrepreneurs in school and college curricula, and the rest of us who simply need to know what is going on.

I hope to prove to you that you can be socially entrepreneurial *whatever* job or role you have (or would like to have), wherever you live, whatever skills and experience you have. That's because, as we shall discover, it's more an outlook or a state of mind than a conventional career or job description. You can engage with social entrepreneurship at a host of different levels. And we need social entrepreneurs who operate in all sorts of situations, inside businesses, public bodies and charities.

So let's start the journey.

Why Jamie Oliver is a social entrepreneur – and why it matters

Every movement needs its heroes. I believe Jamie Oliver has popularised social entrepreneurship in a particularly helpful way and has acted as a catalyst prompting the emerging movement to switch from niche to mainstream. Virtually every country has social entrepreneur heroes emerging, and we shall meet many of them later. Jamie's story is just one example to help us identify the traits of the social entrepreneur in a particular culture.

Many of us feel we know Jamie Oliver almost personally thanks to his TV exposure in over 40 countries and his string of cookery books. For those who don't, here's a potted biography: growing up in an Essex country pub, he became excited by cooking as a young boy, and took early jobs at well-known London establishments the Neal Street Restaurant and the River Café. By 24 he had his first TV series, *The Naked Chef*. The provocative title didn't mean he was actually naked (to some people's disappointment, I seem to recall), but that his style was pared down, in your face, no nonsense. Delivery was rapid-fire and witty, with handfuls of this and a splash of that. He connected with a younger generation than other TV chefs did, but still managed to appeal to all ages. He quickly became a national icon, with an astonishing output of TV series and books. By 25 he was a millionaire.

And then he did something surprising. He set out to prove that he could take a group of young people from disadvantaged backgrounds (homeless, unemployed, fighting drug or alcohol problems) and by a combination of encouragement, abuse and sheer hard work get them to the standard of professional chefs. All in a swanky new London restaurant in which he would invest his own money, and with opening night looming. After overcoming a series of barriers Fifteen opened successfully: people paid good money for the food (and continue to do so) and the Fifteen Foundation subsequently expanded to open new branches in Cornwall, the Netherlands and Australia. There are plans for franchises in New York, South Africa and anywhere that wants one.

Why does this qualify as social entrepreneurship? The business Jamie Oliver has created employs and trains people who would otherwise be unlikely to achieve success in this particular field, or at such a level. What's more, it does so in a way that compromises neither the need to produce a high-quality product paid for by real customers or the need to operate a sustainable business. It is a social enterprise.

But that's not all. Just three years later, Oliver dished up *Jamie's School Dinners*, a project to improve the diet of schoolchildren. The recipe was elegant: one part traditional lobbying campaign (to convince key government and local authority officials of the need for change) to two parts social entrepreneurship. The method was hands-on: Jamie started with an analysis of the business model underlying school meal provision, took it apart, re-engineered it with healthy food and trained the staff at the front line to be able to deliver it. He added a hefty portion of marketing to children and parents alike, both of whom were resistant to change for different reasons. No one who saw it will forget the sight of frustrated parents shoving fast food through gaps in school fences.

In the end, though, Jamie vanquished the turkey twizzler, elevated the matter of school dinners hugely in the public consciousness and demonstrated that an alternative model could be viable. Despite setbacks and erratic progress, he managed to make a genuine impact on children's diet and health across the country.

Of course, all of this makes good TV, attracting the inevitable criticism that it is publicity driven rather than purely socially motivated. And for some people, Oliver's lucrative advertising contract with Sainsbury's has compromised his independence. But do these things really matter if he has helped raise people's awareness of poor nutrition and its effect on children's education?

Jamie Oliver has shown how powerful the social entrepreneur's approach to effecting change can be. He is undoubtedly one of the reasons why so many people are now hailing social entrepreneurship as a revolutionary force for good, and social enterprise as the new business model for the twenty-first century.

All hail the social entrepreneur!

Who is saying this? Politicians of all persuasions, academics and business leaders and opinion-formers.

UK prime minister Gordon Brown's recent book celebrates those many 'everyday heroes' who have inspired him by their commitment to tackling a wide variety of problems. Over a quarter are 'a new generation of social entrepreneurs proving that successful business can benefit communities.' He calls these people 'pathfinders to a better society.'[1]

While there is no love lost between the two leading British political parties, one thing they do agree on is the value of social enterprise. The leader of the opposition, David Cameron, declares that 'In every part of Britain, inspiring social entrepreneurs are pioneering solutions to the complex problems of family breakdown, chaotic home environments, drugs, and low aspiration.'[2]

As US president, George W. Bush surprised some commentators by citing the example of a social entrepreneur in his 2007 State of the Nation address. And former US vice-president Al Gore has hooked up with several social entrepreneurs, as we shall see later.

Academics want to know what makes social entrepreneurs tick and how they do what they do: innovate in difficult circumstances, identify and seize opportunities, make money go further and achieve surprising outcomes.[3]

Business leaders such as Klaus Schwab, the influential founder and convenor of the Davos World Economic Forum, are converts to the idea. But is it possible that one day *all* entrepreneurs will be social entrepreneurs? Is this a revolution or just a load of hype? This book aims to give you the evidence to decide for yourself.

From heroes to ... me?

You may be thinking: these heroic-sounding social entrepreneurs are all very well but how is this relevant to me? I'm a teacher/student/accountant/retired person. Commentator Charlie Leadbeater captures it well:

> Social entrepreneurs find innovative ways to achieve a social mission whether they are working in a local authority, a charity, a large company, a social enterprise or a community group. Social entrepreneurship needs to become a mass activity, practised in many different settings by ordinary people, not just inspirational mavericks.[4]

I know an amazing social entrepreneur who used to be a teacher. It isn't necessarily a barrier; it may even be a springboard. If you're not at school or college now, you were once – and you may be a parent of a student or have some other connection with education. And this is not the moment for cheap jibes at accountants; suffice to say that financial skills are invaluable and there are some entrepreneurial accountants (on the right side of the law too!). Other people don't have the chance to discover their socially entrepreneurial side until they retire.

We certainly need to understand and celebrate the mavericks, the high-profile heroes; but helping social entrepreneurship become a *mass activity* is the greater prize, and my main purpose in writing this book. The revolution is happening at all levels, from the personal to the global.

At a personal level, I believe social entrepreneurship is one of the most exciting experiences working life can offer. You could be trying to set up something that's never been done. You have a higher purpose than churning out commercial products like a sweet brown fizzy liquid. You are aiming to build something that has a life of its own and will last. You will meet some great people along the way. You can feel good about doing good. Heck, you might even win a Nobel Prize! It is a route to fulfilment not for selfish reasons but as a by-product of the work.

However, a mass movement is not just about getting a large number of people to find greater satisfaction in their work. Nor even about bringing all sorts of benefits to our communities. We are talking here about a cultural change with wide implications for the way we run society, do business and organise government.

In communities across the world, people are taking control of their own destinies. Young people turned off by traditional politics seem drawn to social entrepreneurship's DIY approach. Business people realise they can put so much more back into society if they use their business skills as well as their money. Politicians of all persuasions are united in the recognition that social enterprise can help them deliver sustainable change.

Young people are often idealistic, and social enterprise can be an excellent way for them to develop a range of skills and attitudes: teamwork, compassion, business and management skills, presentation, sheer hard graft. Many social enterprises address youth exclusion and disaffection by creating routes back to full participation in society, and in some cases in the operation of the social enterprises themselves. No less than the London Business School believes that promoting a social entrepreneurship culture should be made a priority, especially in schools, to widen participation beyond traditional enterprise teaching, enable young people to realise their potential in the labour market and create opportunities for all.[5] The same research claims that social start-ups are being created at a faster rate than traditional businesses in the UK and are more likely to survive.

These are important and surprising facts. Something's going on. This book tells you what it is and how to be a part of it.

What's in this book

Chapter 2 explores what people think a social entrepreneur is, and goes in search of the personalities and characteristics that make up some of the living, breathing social entrepreneurs out there today.

Chapter 3 is a personal self-assessment tool that will enable you to uncover your own social entrepreneur characteristics.

Chapters 4 to 6 introduce a range of extraordinary ordinary people. They look at what makes four of the world's greatest social entrepreneurs tick; three 'mega social entrepreneurs' who are taking great ideas and multiplying their impact through innovative methods; and others working in a multitude of settings across the globe.

Chapter 7 identifies the seven types of social entrepreneur, looking in detail at the settings in which they operate and the ways that they tailor their methods to achieve maximum impact.

In Chapter 8 we roll up our sleeves and get practical, taking the beermat approach to becoming a social entrepreneur and exploring the basics of entrepreneurial methods to address a social challenge. Then chapter 9 offers careers advice on how to get started.

Chapter 10 looks at where social entrepreneurs are beginning to go next in addressing some of the greatest needs of people and the planet today. It also sets an agenda for some of the pressing priorities we haven't really addressed yet but could, given sufficient support.

By the end of the book I hope you will agree that there are potential social entrepreneurs in all walks of life, from the community to the public and private sector. But many of them lack the awareness, confidence or information to make the switch. Some chance event is often needed to trigger it – but why not choose to explore the possibility as and when it suits you? We conclude with a rousing call to arms for you as a person and us all as a group to achieve our full potential.

There are practical resources and pointers throughout the book and in the appendix. You should find everything you need here to make that decision to get started.

By the end of the book you should:

- Know what social entrepreneurship is
- Recognise a social entrepreneur if you see one
- Find out if you are one
- ... or could be one
- Be aware of what you need to work on
- Know how to get into social entrepreneurship
- Understand the different types
- Know about the wide range of social enterprises operating around the world
- Understand the basics about how to set up your own social enterprise.

2

What is a social entrepreneur?

'A good entrepreneur never gives up.'
Sabeer Bhatia, Hotmail founder

N ot many people know what a social entrepreneur is. It's not a term you hear often, and it can't be said to trip easily off the tongue.

It made its first tentative appearances in academic writing in the 1960s, but was popularised by Bill Drayton, founder of Ashoka (of which more in chapter 5), in the 1980s. Its progress towards wider recognition and use has been patchy. To many people it's an unknown quantity, a bit of a mystery. Even those who use it differ in their opinions and emphases.

So in this chapter we try to get a solid grip on the term and the people it describes, from those who are doing it and those who write about it.

General awareness

To conduct an informal poll for the purposes of this book, I asked people from various walks of life and age groups whether they had heard the term 'social entrepreneur.' If they had, I asked them the first thing that came into their head on hearing it, how they would define it, and whether they could name any social entrepreneurs.

Less than a quarter had even heard of the term, and surprisingly few of them could hazard a guess at what it might mean. Others who said they had heard it had a range of misconceptions. One person felt the term was contradictory, another that it was elitist. The most amusing view was that it was a 'sociable' entrepreneur! Some quality newspaper readers had seen articles on the subject and were able to name Anita Roddick, Jamie Oliver and Tim Smit as examples of social entrepreneurs. Among others who had heard of the term, many picked entrepreneurs who are known for their philanthropy such as Bill Gates and Sir Richard Branson. Most seemed to pick any well-known entrepreneur or celebrity: Sir Alan Sugar, James Dyson, and even David Beckham and Elton John. So there is clearly a gap in many people's understanding of the subject.

In a larger-scale survey on social entrepreneurship and social enterprise, the British government was taken aback to discover that only one in four people know what a social enterprise is.[1] To address this lack, it launched an awareness-raising programme that includes ambassadors and incorporation of the subject into the school curriculum.

It's clear from this that there is a huge disconnection between the aspirations of practitioners and advocates of social entrepreneurship and the perceptions of the general public. With a bit of prompting, many people can understand what social entrepreneurship is about and engage with it at some level. But how many believe they can participate in it? And how many could actually do so? Surely the numbers must be tiny?

A variation on entrepreneurship?

To answer these questions, we need to go back a few steps. Let's start by looking briefly at the term 'entrepreneur.' We hear about these people all the time. What's your reaction when you hear the word? Do certain names and images spring to mind? Do you see them as good, bad or a bit of both? It's often said that people in the States admire entrepreneurs while in Britain we are more likely to envy or resent them.

The origins of the word may help us to understand why this attitude still prevails. 'Entrepreneur' derives from the French *entreprendre* (to undertake), which in turn comes from *entre* (between) and *prendre* (to take), giving a sense of a trader who 'goes between' and takes something out of a deal. When the term was first used by French economic writers as early as the 1700s, it already embodied the idea that the person starting their undertaking or venture takes risks, in recognition of which they are entitled to their 'take.'

Entrepreneurs get a mixed press. Let's think about the positive side first. Some of their achievements include providing products and services that people need, creating jobs and opportunities, and generating wealth. Some of the negative associations might be excess, greed, arrogance, inequality, ruthlessness. When you think of Richard Branson, Alan Sugar, Donald Trump and so on, what would your assessment be?

Research has shown that most entrepreneurs are not motivated purely by financial gain or risk-taking for their own sake, but by the need for achievement. They regard money as a validation of their market strategy. And they accept challenges only when they perceive that there is a reasonable chance of success, in which their skill is the main determinant.[2]

But is entrepreneurship still tarnished by negative connotations? Is it sometimes too harshly judged? If so, can it be redeemed? Here's how one influential entrepreneur with an ethical dimension – the late Anita Roddick, founder of the Body Shop – defined herself and her mission.

1. The *vision* of something new and belief in it that's so strong that it becomes a reality.
2. A touch of *craziness* – a dream that is almost a madness because you have seen something that others don't.
3. The ability to stand out from the crowd because entrepreneurs act *instinctively* on what they see, think and feel.
4. The ability to have *ideas* constantly bubbling up inside until they are forced out by the pressure of creative tension (but ideas are nothing unless someone can make them reality).
5. Pathological *optimism*, believing that anything is possible.
6. A covert understanding that you don't have to know *how* to do something. It's not skill or money but *knowledge* that is the answer, wherever it may be found.
7. *Streetwise* skills – getting stuck in, looking for the way to achieve change.
8. *Creativity* – tapping into the mystery of this unique human quality.
9. The ability to *mix* all these together effectively – keep asking questions and knocking on doors, seek opinions – then make up your own mind. Doing, not theory, is what counts.
10. Every entrepreneur is a good *storyteller* – this defines your differences.[3]

These are striking descriptions, and they give a profound insight into the entrepreneurial mind. A more succinct (if drier) definition distilled from decades of research and analysis is offered by entrepreneurship experts Bill Bolton and John Thompson:

> 'An entrepreneur is a person who habitually creates and innovates to build something of recognized value around perceived opportunities.'[4]

Bolton and Thompson's research has looked at both what entrepreneurs *do* and what they are *like*. In terms of personality, entrepreneurs will often be confident, optimistic, compulsive, courageous, persistent, extroverted. They will exhibit high energy and drive, urgency, imagination and initiative. They will be able to persuade and maybe inspire; focus on outcomes and results; engage the support of others; and build support for new initiatives.[5] Bolton and Thompson make a crucial distinction between:

- Talents – the abilities we are largely born with
- Temperament – which determines whether those talents flourish or not and
- Technique – the skills which can be learned or acquired.[6]

They distil all these different features into a set of 'entrepreneur character themes':[7]

- Successful entrepreneurs are able to stay **focused** on key business issues, initiating strategic actions and maintaining the momentum of change and growth
- The importance of a clear and winning strategy, one which promises and delivers something valuable for all stakeholders, but especially the customers: competitive **advantage**
- **Creativity** and innovation in action
- The desire of certain people with a strong **ego** to make a difference with the things they do and achieve. They are agents of change
- People are at the heart of business success and must be motivated and led effectively. Successful businesses are dependent on effective **teams**.

The first letters of each of the highlighted words make a useful mnemonic: FACET. Each facet is an aspect of the whole, and they should all be present to some degree in the entrepreneur. There's just one more element in Bolton and Thompson's full set of facets that make up the social entrepreneur – can you guess what it is? No, it's not a trick question. You might call it the 'S factor': the **social** facet transforms the others to make the social entrepreneur. We'll return to the facets framework as part of the self-assessment tool in chapter 3.

Opinion differs on the relative proportion of people that exhibit these entrepreneurial characteristics. Estimates of the *potentially* entrepreneurial range from 40% of the population in the US to 10-15% in the UK. However, in the UK the share of people who are *being* genuinely entrepreneurial may be as low as 1%.[8] The reason for the difference, Bolton and Thompson believe, is down to whether a culture and its education system encourage or discourage entrepreneurship. There is a simple test: when a young person chooses an entrepreneurial rather than a traditional working or academic route, is it a surprise and an exception? Or is it expected and encouraged?

Another survey puts total entrepreneurial activity in the UK at 6.2% of the adult population, with socially entrepreneurial activity at half that level (even using a very broad definition of social project engagement).[9] It's not zero – but there's clearly room for growth.

Where the social entrepreneur comes in

So where does this apparently rare creature, the social entrepreneur, fit into the world? The conventional business model says you make as much money as possible (often described as 'maximising shareholder value'):

- First, without doing anything illegal (or at least getting caught)
- Then without doing anything harmful ('do no evil,' as Google says)
- If necessary (whether for conscience, guilt or PR), give away a small amount of your profit to good causes or charitable foundations
- Don't forget to behave ethically in your business operations: produce an annual corporate social responsibility report saying how nice you are to work for, how well you treat your suppliers and customers, and how carefully you look after the environment.

Social entrepreneurship turns this on its head: you do business in order to solve social problems. You solve social problems by doing business. The business is the solution.

But it's not just in business that the social entrepreneur is rewriting the rulebook. In the public sector the conventional approach says that we need to raise taxes from businesses and individuals to spend on democratically agreed priorities, so we need companies and employees to work hard and operate profitably so that we have enough money to distribute for the public good. If we as a government spend this money on a national basis but with regional and local variations, we should achieve the optimum combination of efficiency (value for money) and effectiveness (impact). Unfortunately there is a lot of evidence that the theory doesn't work so well in practice, especially in the mind-bogglingly complex and costly areas of health and education.

Social entrepreneurship claims (and governments increasingly agree) that one of the best ways to make services genuinely responsive at a local level – whether in health, education, recycling or transport – is to allow social enterprises to deliver them. Privatisation is too extreme in many cases, but social enterprise has the right philosophical and practical approach to provide efficiency with equity.

To complete the picture, the traditional charity approach works in the gaps left between private business and the public sector, picking up those who fall through the net and generally relying on handouts from the public, businesses or government, or all three. Perhaps the most entrepreneurial a charity might get is to run a charity shop. This is not intended as a criticism: charities do a great job and create many social benefits, but they are really about giving the public more reasons to donate money.

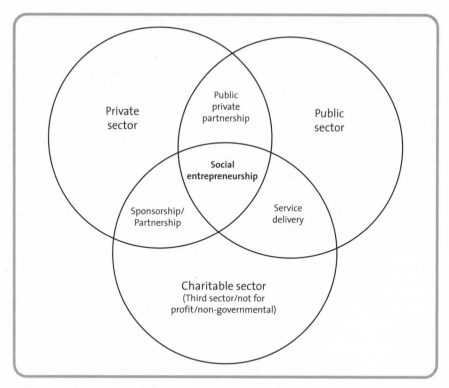

The shifting balance between the three sectors

Social entrepreneurship challenges this mindset by insisting that dependence on grants and gifts can carry its own risks. Instead, we need to look wherever possible for ways to generate our own sustainable sources of income and means to grow. This could be achieved in a variety of ways: charging for services, building parallel or cross-subsidy businesses (where one supports the other financially), or ideally integrating your business and your mission by developing an enterprise that serves both at the same time.

What's happening now is that the traditional boundaries are blurring, and social entrepreneurship is emerging somewhere between the old established categories.

Most countries are familiar with the gradual privatisation of public services – what we might identify as the first big crossover between the three sectors. And government has for a long time paid some charities (also sometimes known as third sector, not-for-profit or non-governmental organisations) to run public services. But social entrepreneurship is a messier business. On the one hand, it's all the more exciting for it; on the other, because it's not a single specific thing that can be easily categorised, it hasn't really entered popular consciousness yet. This has led to confusion over what it is, as well as criticism. As trend analyst and think-tank guru Charlie Leadbeater observes:

> 'Critics allege social entrepreneurship is a vague idea. On the contrary, social entrepreneurship has grown because it is so plastic, ambiguous and adaptable. It is a promiscuous idea that can work in many different settings.'[10]

His use of the word 'promiscuous' is an intriguing way of capturing a sense of the challenging, controversial and risky nature of this sometimes provocative activity. It confronts the status quo and people's view of how things should be. Or if you prefer a culinary analogy, it's like the effect of yeast on a batch of dough or the fermentation of beer: something capable of endless growth and regeneration. Wherever it reaches, it has an amazing and disproportionate – but sometimes unsettling – transformational effect.

So who has been affected by it? We've already looked at Jamie Oliver's social entrepreneurship journey. Here are some more examples.

New heroes of social entrepreneurship

Social entrepreneurs can come from unlikely places. Bill Gates made his fortune by selling us software, and is now finding an important outlet for his money (and perhaps his conscience) through his charitable foundation addressing malaria, HIV/AIDS and tuberculosis. Another of the world's richest men, Warren Buffett, has joined him, pitching in a cool US$30 billion on top of Bill's billions. You might think that Gates is just the latest recruit to the old school of ruthless capitalists who reach a certain point in their lives and then choose to atone for their single-minded pursuit of profit through generous philanthropy. But I would argue that there is a crucial difference. Gates is applying his own entrepreneurial skills to the solution of the need, which is why he has attracted Buffett's backing. Instead of handing over his money and delegating managers to spend it according to his wishes, he has given up the day job to run his trust himself according to business principles. As I see it, Bill (version 2.0) is becoming a social entrepreneur.

Jeff Skoll touches most of our lives through eBay, but as an idealist this young billionaire is now enjoying the opportunity to let his social entrepreneur side flourish. His Skoll Foundation funds the Skoll Centre for Social Entrepreneurship at the Oxford University Business School, as well as a film company, Participant Productions, which makes movies and documentaries that promote social values.

The founders of Google, finding themselves multi-billionaires in their early 30s, decided to apply their entrepreneurial skills not just to 'doing no evil' but actively doing good through their socially entrepreneurial foundation Google.org. As they explained in their letter to shareholders:

'We hope that someday this institution will eclipse Google itself in overall world impact by ambitiously applying innovation and significant resources to the largest of the world's problems.'[11]

Then there are public-sector social entrepreneurs. Take Geoff Mulgan, former director of the policy unit at 10 Downing Street, where the unthinkable was thought and radical ideas were generated for government consideration in social exclusion, welfare, family issues, urban issues and government reform. Ten years ago it was inconceivable that every three-year-old would have a free nursery place, every child an asset endowment at birth and every worker the right to a minimum wage. The fact that all these policies are now in place is at least partly down to Mulgan's vision. He has since moved into the charity sector, where he aims to keep innovation going at the Young Foundation.

Bob Geldof has used a socially entrepreneurial approach in the charity sector, repeatedly coming up with innovative ways to raise both money and awareness in tackling global poverty. He uses his business acumen, industry contacts and immense drive to mastermind landmark events like Live Aid, Live 8 and Band Aid ('Do They Know It's Christmas?'), combining these efforts with behind-the-scenes political savvy to lobby for change as well as funding.

Social entrepreneurs are also active in the direct delivery of development projects in poor countries. Muhammad Yunus, the first social entrepreneur to win a Nobel Prize, was working as an academic economist in rural Bangladesh in the 1970s when he identified the need for affordable credit to enable poor labourers to earn enough from their businesses to escape poverty. He lent the money himself and step by step, learning and innovating all the way and overcoming every obstacle in his path, he built a bank. We'll look in detail at Muhammad Yunus and others later to pull out lessons as well as to find inspiration and a sense of challenge.

But the reason I think these stories can accurately be described as both messy and exciting is that it is highly unlikely that any of these people planned their careers to evolve in the way they did. Yunus didn't know that his initial loan experiment would end up as a major banking institution. Even Bill Gates, who doesn't come across as a man who leaves so much as his choice of breakfast cereal to chance, is unlikely to have woken up in his late teens and said 'I'm going to make a stack of money, then give a huge proportion of it away – oh, and do so in a way which uses my business skills.' (Actually, maybe he did...) No, it emerged as a possibility once he had reached a certain point, and he decided to pursue it. The opportunity was to combine his entrepreneurial skills with his social passion – and his money.

Other messy and exciting social entrepreneur stories we'll discover include a toilet entrepreneur in east Asia and people who work in slums and tackle the world's most difficult diseases. These are people who literally get their hands dirty, and change people's lives in the most amazing way in the process. You have been warned!

Social entrepreneurs from A to Z

In virtually every country on earth from Afghanistan to Zimbabwe, people who set out to be or would be recognised as social entrepreneurs have started businesses to save a village post office, to develop multimillion-pound buildings for community use, to plug gaps in market or government provision, or to take on big businesses in transport, finance and healthcare. Here is a list of just ten to give you an idea of the breadth and variety of activity pursued by contemporary social entrepreneurs.

Country	Person/organisation	Field/achievement
Afghanistan	Sakena Yacoobi, Afghan Institute of Learning	Education: teaching 350,000 women and children; training 10,000 teachers
Australia	Bill Lawson, founder, Beacon Foundation	Economic development: reducing school-leaver unemployment in part of Tasmania from 30% to zero
Brazil	Joaquim de Melo Neto Segundo, People's Bank	Finance: setting up slum-based community bank with alternative currency
China	Wu Qing, Practical Skills Training Centre for Rural Women, and women's magazine	Gender equality: helping more than 2,600 rural women and girls learn skills for economic and political independence
Germany	Andreas Heinecke, Dialogue in the Dark	Human rights / disability: empowering 4,000 blind people to teach sighted people
India	Kousalya Periasamy, India Positive Women Network	Health: establishing grassroots support network for 2.5 million women with HIV/AIDS
Nicaragua	Catalina Ruiz, Learning in Community	Ecotourism / economic development: engaging visitors in experiences with poor communities
Poland	Jarek Dominiak, Individual Investors' Association	Economic development: setting up local investment clubs to help citizens understand and participate in the economic transition from communism
United States	Michael Brown, Alan Khazei, City Year	Youth / civic engagement: one-year community volunteering programme for young people
Zimbabwe	Lydia Chabata, AZTREC	Environment: tree planting and ecological sustainability project

This is a very disparate list – so what is it that makes all these people social entrepreneurs?

Entrepreneur bad, social entrepreneur good?

Social entrepreneurs have to live – for better or worse – with all the baggage that being an entrepreneur entails. Does the word 'social' exempt them from the negatives? Does it matter? Let's unpack the phrase for a moment.

The introduction of the word 'social' transforms the entrepreneur's whole rationale. If the conventional entrepreneur's success is measured primarily by profit (the financial outputs or 'bottom line' of any business), the social entrepreneur's interest lies in social as well as monetary outputs. Note the words 'as well as.' The financial side can't be ignored. This has led to the characterisation of social enterprise as a business with *two* bottom lines, financial and social. Success or failure depends on the balance between the two. (Some social businesses include environmental impact as an equal consideration and thus operate with three bottom lines. This can make successful operation even more challenging, as we'll see later.)

For now, though, let's just look at social outputs. What are they?

Jamie Oliver's Fifteen restaurants aim to train and employ excluded young people to operate a successful business. Successful is defined as profit-making – a restaurant that customers like and keep returning to.

Emmaus gives homeless people a bed, companionship and a job in a furniture recycling business, on the condition that they come off welfare payments and give up drugs and alcohol. Cambridge University measured all the social outputs from its local Emmaus community and costed them at a saving of over £600,000 a year to the public purse: that's money saved on welfare, medical attention, and intervention from the criminal justice system (it costs around £70,000 to keep someone in prison for a year).[12] More importantly, Emmaus is contributing to society through the social business it operates, sustainably and with no need for grants. Emmaus communities are growing across Europe thanks to the pioneering work of their founder, the late Abbé Pierre, a priest and social entrepreneur.

To paraphrase E. F. Schumacher, enterprises like these seem to be doing business as if people matter most. It starts with a need: to get young people or the homeless into meaningful work. Or an opportunity: I already train the best candidates to become chefs, so why not see if I can extend that to people who come from a challenging background?

In the simplest terms, social entrepreneurs apply business methods to social problems. One of the easiest places to identify social entrepreneurs in action is in the emerging social enterprise movement. It occupies an interesting space in the economy, as the diagram illustrates.

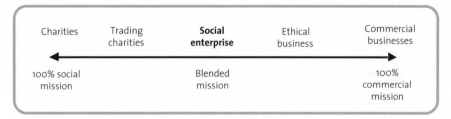

Charities	Trading charities	**Social enterprise**	Ethical business	Commercial businesses
100% social mission		Blended mission		100% commercial mission

The charity / social enterprise / commercial continuum

Starting at the left end you have the majority of traditional charities (or 'non-profits' in the US), which are almost entirely reliant on gifts from the public and sometimes government. They are experts at fundraising through events, mailshots, cold-calling and street collections. The biggest operators among them are the aid and children's charities, whose fundraising methods are well suited to their 'heart-string' causes.

Moving to the right we find a group that often mixes similar funding approaches with delivery of public services under contract to local authorities or central government: care homes, some health services, transport for the disabled. Some of these tend to be characterised as the 'voluntary and community sector,' though there are a lot of large charities in there too. Others have trading arms – usually charity shops but also catalogues and merchandise – and can be classified as a basic form of social enterprise.

At the opposite extreme lie the purely commercial businesses. Most of these do give money away, but some have adopted the practice only recently in response to peer and customer pressure.

Moving towards the centre, next come the ethical businesses: the Body Shop, Ben and Jerry's ice-cream franchises, Triodos Bank, Innocent Smoothies, The Ethical Property Company. These are definitely commercial concerns, but their market niche is based on delivering an ethical product, often by charging premium prices or offering a slightly lower than average return on investment.

Finally, in the mid point between the two poles we find social enterprises. The perfect example is 100% self-sufficient, generating all its revenue from providing a product or service, possibly to a group of customers who have a specific need or are at some disadvantage, and possibly employing people with these needs or disadvantages in the delivery process. When a social enterprise makes a surplus it reinvests it in the company or community rather than distributing it privately.

FRC (formerly the Furniture Resource Centre) is a good example. This Liverpool-based company employs long-term unemployed people to collect and refurbish furniture which it then sells at affordable prices to customers who can't afford new goods. Add in the bonus of a positive impact on the environment through recycling, and you have the perfect social enterprise model. Despite that, FRC has been through many ups and downs, as two people closely involved in its early years, Liam Black and Jeremy Nicholls, freely admit in their book *There's No Business like Social Business*.[13] Given the fierce competition FRC experiences, there is no guarantee it will survive, but Black and Nicholls suggest that the business is at least wise to that, and describe how it has walked the tightrope to balance social and financial priorities.

It's estimated there are at least 55,000 social enterprises in the UK. They comprise a fascinating mix of development trusts, community enterprises, housing associations, social firms, leisure trusts and co-operative businesses. Their business is tackling market failures: identifying needs that are not being met by businesses either because they do not perceive the opportunity, or can't see a way of making an adequate profit from it. Many have their origins in the Victorian era, when mutual provision mushroomed in response to industrialisation and the emergence of new social problems. While charities and the state have traditionally offered help for those falling through the safety net, the other way of looking at things is to ask why people are falling in the first place.

Social enterprises are ideally suited to creating meaningful employment for those who would otherwise struggle to get a job in the open market: people who have been out of work for a long time, or have a disability or mental health problem. Some social enterprise jobs are a stepping-stone to the open market; others are more permanent, and are gradually replacing the old 'supported employment' schemes set up by post-war governments to occupy disabled people with achievable tasks. As these schemes are scaled back, social enterprises are stepping in to provide a wider variety of creative and satisfying supportive work environments.

Other social enterprises employ people with no particular support needs but are on a mission to make some aspect of society better. So Yunus's Grameen Bank is not primarily a sympathetic employer, but a bank with a social mission.

Not all social entrepreneurs set up or operate social enterprises. All social entrepreneurs want to bring about social change, but some adopt business-like income-generation strategies and some seek other approaches to sustainability.

A definition offered at the Skoll World Forum on Social Entrepreneurship may help to settle the dispute. Take a deep breath:

> *The social entrepreneur should be understood as someone who targets an unfortunate but stable equilibrium that causes the neglect, marginalization, or suffering of a segment of humanity; who brings to bear on this situation his or her*

inspiration, direct action, creativity, courage, and fortitude; and who aims for and ultimately effects the establishment of a new stable equilibrium that secures permanent benefit for the targeted group and society at large.[14]

To translate: they see a bad situation, envisage a better one, and work out how to get from here to there. It is a broader view than simple market failure: it is about whole systems or societal failure. To tackle it, social entrepreneurs do a variety of things including setting up social enterprises, ethical businesses and social-change institutions – or even aiming to influence mainstream businesses, as we shall see later.

Hallmarks of the social entrepreneur

Liam Black and Jeremy Nicholls have spent a lot of time training and developing social entrepreneurs to achieve greater impact. They describe the typical social entrepreneur as being:

- Passionate about their enterprises and the social and environmental purposes
- Ideologically and sectorally promiscuous – meaning they network far and wide, seek to learn from wherever they can and are excellent at adapting what they learn into their own businesses; with the private sector increasingly a source of innovation
- Restlessly driven and ruthless in pursuing their objectives
- Curious
- Skilled at creating great teams around them.[15]

The key difference between a social and a private entrepreneur is the idealism that prompts someone to opt for the former rather than the latter. Black and Nicholls quote one young social entrepreneur who describes it as a 'balance of idealism and realism.'[16]

So much for what they are like, but what do social entrepreneurs actually do? Charlie Leadbeater identifies these actions as characteristic of the social entrepreneur:

- Identify under-utilised resources – people, buildings and equipment – and find ways of putting them to use to satisfy unmet social needs
- Create impressive schemes with virtually no resources
- Effectively communicate a mission to inspire staff, users and partners
- Focus on that mission rather than the pursuit of profit or shareholder value
- Promote health, welfare and well-being.[17]

When you see lists of these characteristics written down on paper, they often look more formidable than they really are. It's unlikely anyone ever saw such a list and thought 'Hey, that sounds like me, better get stuck in straight away,' or spotted one or two qualities that they lacked and booked training courses to rectify the deficiencies. I'm not providing the list as a set of prerequisites, but as a stimulus for thought, to encourage you to take a fresh look at yourself and ask what else might be lying undiscovered within you. If only one characteristic chimes with you, that may be the very thing that sets you on the way to achieving something incredible.

One phrase that has been used of social entrepreneurs is 'ordinary people with extraordinary abilities.' They often start with no conventional business background and simply by rising to a challenge end up developing initiatives that are surprisingly business-like and entrepreneurial. They may be church ministers, community workers, sports players.[18] If there is a unifying theme it has to do with what business guru and social entrepreneur Patrick Dixon has called the drive to *build a better world*.[19] Although this impulse is common to many societies and institutions, the social entrepreneur's contribution is expressed through the development of creative, sustainable responses to social needs.

As other commentators put it, 'What distinguishes social entrepreneurship is the primacy of social benefit.'[20] It's about quality of life, and in some cases life itself. It extends from basic needs for water, shelter, food and healthcare to education, work, the arts, sport – supplying whatever is lacking to create a better community or society.

When people work together in socially entrepreneurial ways to make life better for themselves and their fellow citizens they are building something that is more precious than can be measured in purely financial terms. They are creating what economists call *social capital*. This is about trust, relationships, mutuality – building the fabric of society. Some see it as a whole new world, the social economy.[21]

These ideas should become more tangible when we look at more detailed case studies in chapters 4, 5 and 6. You can almost *feel* the social fabric being repaired and rewoven.

Social entrepreneurs are simply people who are trying to build a better world. The term may be ugly, but it does the job. It captures the essence of combining the social mission and the entrepreneurial approach.

The key characteristics of a social entrepreneur are drive, commitment to a cause, and the ability to see the need and the means to address it, acquire the resources (financial, human, physical), and develop the team or organisation to deliver the response. But being a social entrepreneur has more to do with your state of mind than your specific skills. At the heart is

How I became a social entrepreneur

As a kid I was fascinated by maps and travel. Not surprisingly, I ended up doing geography at university. But as well as studying maps, mountains and glaciers, I also got a massive social and political awakening to the needs of the world. My gut reaction was to go into overseas development work of some kind. But I realised I had no practical skills to offer and would have to retrain.

I met an entrepreneurial community activist who worked with inner-city churches on local regeneration. He challenged me to consider 'the third world on my doorstep' – perhaps not the most sensitive description of deprived British communities, but it was the turning point for me. I helped him with research on the most effective community-based responses to unemployment and poverty, an experience that sent me travelling around the country on a shoestring, usually hitch-hiking, often with a folding bike, and relying on the hospitality of contacts everywhere.

One of the projects, at the Sheffield YMCA, turned out to have such a compelling pull that I moved there to help set it up. Overnight I changed from being a dispassionate researcher to an engaged participant. And it was an exhilarating experience, living in the midst of the problems, meeting unemployed people and learning about their pain and hopes. The project got off to a successful start, providing training in life skills to unemployed young people.

By now I was totally committed to tackling the issue of unemployment. I couldn't bear seeing people who were able and willing to work being denied the opportunity. It was so cruel, yet surely not beyond human ingenuity to solve.

I realised that I had to dedicate my life to eradicating this scourge. I felt the best thing I could do was to study unemployment in great detail, so I did a PhD in Sheffield on the life histories of young men who had oscillated between low-paid work, unemployment and government-sponsored training schemes. That was fine, and deepened my understanding and motivation. But academia didn't seem a good way to make a difference; it was hard to get people to listen, and I hated teaching!

So I went back into the charity sector, to an enterprise called Citylife that was set up to get people and companies to invest in tackling unemployment in Britain's cities. I've been there ever since. It's a social business that aims to become self-sufficient and achieve huge social impact. It has taught me what it takes to be a social entrepreneur: creativity and determination in getting a project up and running, flexibility and ingenuity in solving myriad problems along the way, and tenacity in keeping the vision going and sharing it with lots of other people. It is not until you are involved in a social enterprise that you realise how much its success depends on a huge range of contributions from funders, trustees, staff, networks and many other people of goodwill.

My journey has been in turn thrilling and exhausting, but I wouldn't have had it any other way. It's hard to predict the future when you are treading new ground every day – but that's one of the joys because you feel deep down that if you succeed you could be making history. Already thousands of people are in work or business because of Citylife. And if we achieve even a fraction of our vision the world will be a better place. You can't ask for greater job satisfaction than that.

the desire to tackle social issues and to do so by creating a sustainable income stream.

■ ■ ■

Social entrepreneurs come in all shapes and sizes. Some are national treasures, others technical and strategic (but obscure and unknown), and yet others ordinary people who have stumbled into social enterprise and found that they too are social entrepreneurs.

Many social entrepreneurs set up social enterprises, so if you want to observe them in their natural habitat look for the founders or drivers of a social business you know. There may be other social entrepreneurs in there too, not just the leaders. And there are social entrepreneurs lurking elsewhere in the community, still to be discovered. Some work strategically in big businesses, local authorities and large charities to bring about catalytic change. We'll see more examples of all these types throughout the book.

Your initial reaction to all this may be: I could never do any of these things. But every social entrepreneur has to start somewhere – the journey of a thousand miles starts with a single step, and all that. However focused and driven the people in this book may seem now, chances are that they weren't like that at the outset, but only got that way once the cause had got under their skin.

You may never have done any of the things we've looked at in this chapter, and perhaps you feel daunted by the very thought. How do you know if you are the kind of person who might have what it takes? This is what chapter 3 is about: techniques to identify your own potential as a social entrepreneur, and how to develop it.

Pause for reflection and action

■ Do these examples leave you feeling daunted or excited and energised?
■ Can you think of any social entrepreneurs you know personally, or have heard about in your area?
■ What makes them stand out?
■ Can you think of a social issue that might benefit from the approaches discussed in this chapter?

3

Could I be a social entrepreneur?

'Most people have jobs that are too small for their spirit.'

Studs Terkel,
US writer and historian

I t is easier to recognise a social entrepreneur by what they do than by their personality type. But what if someone hasn't yet started out as a social entrepreneur – can you test for their potential? Or if they have started and are struggling, can you find the reason? This chapter aims to identify relevant traits in your personality, as well as weaknesses that you can work on or at least be aware of. If you are already a social entrepreneur, or are interested in supporting other social entrepreneurs, I hope this chapter will provide useful insights into ways to identify and develop the characteristics you need.

Can anyone be entrepreneurial? Is it a trait you are born with, and later discover (or not)? Or can it be learned? Opinions differ, as we have seen. Successful entrepreneurs sometimes think that anyone can be one. Indeed, one recent bestseller – *Anyone Can Do It* by Duncan Bannatyne – is based on exactly this unlikely premise.[1] Maybe anyone can, in theory. But given the risks, maybe not everyone should try in practice. People who have seen it all go wrong are more cautious. Too much can depend on it: your house, your marriage, your health, even your life.

With social entrepreneurship, though, the risks are usually lower. You can try it out around your existing job, if you have one. You can mix it into your portfolio of activities. It can begin as voluntary work. And you shouldn't have to risk your own money or put your house on the line (although some people do) so the overall risk is perhaps not so paralysing.

Remember too that being an entrepreneur is a matter of degree: how enterprising you can be, and how far you exhibit the tendencies we explored in the previous chapter. If, as Bolton and Thompson suggest, the entrepreneur is a mixture of talent, temperament and technique, techniques can be learned, talents can be developed, and temperament can be managed to allow talents and technique to flourish.[2]

I believe social entrepreneurship has a paradoxical aspect. On the one hand, it is more daunting in some respects than conventional entrepreneurship because of the challenge of meeting social and perhaps environmental goals as well as generating sustainable income. On the other hand, because practitioners are chiefly motivated by responding to real human need, they enjoy certain advantages: extra determination, opportunities for partnership that would not exist in the private sector, wider sources of initial funding to cushion the start-up process, and a more sympathetic operating environment overall.

Now it's time to get personal. What about *you*? Could you be a social entrepreneur? What are your skills and aptitudes? What would you need to work on?

Here is your chance to assess yourself as a potential social entrepreneur. By taking analyses of the characteristics of social entrepreneurs from several different authors and my own research and combining them with elements of a proven entrepreneur assessment methodology, I have developed a new self-assessment process. It explores three areas that taken together give you a balanced view of your strengths and weaknesses:

1. What sort of person are you?
2. Are you or could you be entrepreneurial?
3. What is the strength of your social motivation?

In answering the questions, be honest with yourself. Don't try to work out what they are trying to get you to reveal; it isn't always obvious and you might delude yourself about your true characteristics – hardly a good basis for the self-understanding we are trying to achieve. The questions are not designed to be scored in any scientific manner, but to help you feel your way and make a broad judgement about yourself.

1. What sort of person are you?

Have you ever taken a personality test? Are you aware of your main characteristics or do you take life as it comes? Has anyone ever said 'You're so …? (Focus on the positive examples!)

Measuring personality traits, characteristics and strengths is big business. Psychometric testing, as it is called, is used to identify suitable careers for young people or those returning to work, and increasingly by employers to screen potential recruits. Many different tests are available, and we shall review some of them later. But for now, let's start with the following list.

In each case you are invited to assess yourself very simply. Do you identify with the characteristic in question? If so, you could use a tick, or maybe a double tick if it sounds exactly like you, or a question mark if you aren't sure. You may also want to mark those you feel are definitely *not* you. But concentrate on finding those that jump out at you – 'That's me!'

So do you see yourself, or do others see you, as any of the following?

Are you...	Sample statement	Yes / no / maybe
Extrovert	I would say on balance I'm an outgoing person – or capable of being so when necessary.	Very
Passionate	When something is important to me, I can become animated and enthusiastic about it.	Very
Proactive	I prefer to make things happen rather than let them happen to me.	½ + ½
Persistent	I am tenacious in pursuit of a goal or the completion of an important task.	yes
Optimistic	I tend to take a positive view of how a situation will turn out even if others despair of it.	very
Relational	I am a people person and can build links with different types of people naturally.	very
Self-confident	I tend to believe that my character or abilities will be enough to get me through most situations.	yes
Pragmatic	I am naturally able to take the practical steps needed to achieve a result, I can be flexible, and I don't feel everything has to be perfect.	yes
Creative	I like coming up with new ideas, solutions to problems and fresh thinking on existing challenges.	yes
Trustworthy	I feel I can be trusted by others and I think they feel the same.	yes
Motivated	I am driven by a purpose, whether in specific tasks or overall.	most of the time
Responsible	Others tend to look to me to take responsibility when organisation or leadership is required, even if I'm not a formal leader.	yes

Why have we started with this list? Well, these are all qualities that people have seen in social entrepreneurs, and that social entrepreneurs have seen in each other.[3] It's interesting that they are not particularly unusual or distinctive in themselves, but would be useful in many settings whether entrepreneurial or not. Good managers (corporate or football) would have many or most of them, and you would hope to find them in teachers and healthcare workers, restaurant staff and other people-facing roles.

Don't panic if you recognise only a handful of these traits in yourself. Very few people would have them all. And remember that we are looking for *potential*: there may be qualities where you aren't confident enough to give yourself a tick now, but know you want to develop in yourself. These characteristics are not necessarily fixed. Researchers observe that they can change over time, and people can adopt them in response to particular role requirements.[4]

And if you don't trust your own ability to make these judgements – perhaps you are too harsh on yourself, or can't resist giving the 'right' answer – then ask yourself how other people might rate you, or get a friend or relative to fill in the table for you. Then set this list aside while we look at the entrepreneurial dimension.

2. Are you or could you be entrepreneurial?

You may have already been successful in business or as an entrepreneur, in which case you will have a head start here. But the point is to identify *potential* entrepreneurial characteristics, which is harder to do if you haven't taken part in formal business activity so far in your life.

When entrepreneurship experts Bill Bolton and John Thompson devised the facets framework described in the previous chapter, they drew on decades of research by the Gallup organisation on human characteristics. Gallup boiled down the myriad identifiable traits into 12 entrepreneurial 'life themes':[5]

Dedication	Consumed by a goal or purpose
Focus	Discriminates and targets
Profit orientation	Advantage focused
Ego drive	Wants to make a recognised difference
Urgency	No time to waste, must take action now
Courage	Determined in the face of adversity
Activator	Wants to make it happen
Opportunity	Sees possibilities not problems
Creativity	Buzzing with ideas
Expertise orientation	Knows own limits and finds experts
Team	Gets the right people together
Individualised perception	Sees and uses strengths in others

Gallup regard the most essential themes for the entrepreneur as creativity, profit orientation (advantage), courage and focus, in that order.[6] Bolton and Thompson comment that many of the themes overlap or work together, such as courage and focus, for example.

Here I intend to concentrate mainly on focus, advantage and creativity as the core of the entrepreneurial character. These are themes that anyone can exhibit, regardless of whether they have ever worked in business.

A. Focus

If you have a strong focus, according to Bolton and Thompson, you can lock onto a target, concentrate and not lose sight of critical issues. Someone who is focused has a sense of urgency, doesn't procrastinate, isn't easily distracted, and has a desire to make things happen and complete tasks. These characteristics aren't exclusive to the entrepreneur, but according to Bolton and Thompson, it isn't possible to be an entrepreneur without them.[7]

Here are some questions to reflect on.[8]

	Yes/ no/ maybe
Can you focus on important tasks, targets or deadlines when they arise?	yes
Do you prefer action to talking?	I like planning
Do you feel you work hard most of the time, or at least when necessary?	yes
Can you identify the things that really matter?	yes
How many of the tasks that you start do you complete?	most

The point of asking yourself these questions is as follows:

- If deadlines make you panic and become ineffective you may struggle when you are under pressure instead of being decisive.
- There is nothing wrong with discussion, but an entrepreneur values action more than endless debate.
- Hard work doesn't make you an entrepreneur, but a dislike of hard work can prevent you from becoming one. Focusing on a task is bound to involve putting in effort at some point.
- The ability to set goals, prioritise and then concentrate is essential.
- Entrepreneurs need to be good at finishing tasks off rather than simply moving on to the next exciting challenge.

In the social entrepreneur, the focus is on the social challenge or problem to be overcome. The most successful social entrepreneurs are, as one vivid description puts it, 'married to a vision.'[9] Craig Dearden-Phillips cites research by Charlotte Chambers and Fiona Edwards-Stuart for the School for Social Entrepreneurs[10] that confirms the importance of focus for the social entrepreneur, but warns of the possible danger that it can lead to inflexibility and an inability to adapt to new situations.

So, in the light of your initial reactions and the comments above, do you agree with this statement?

> **Yes, on balance I can focus when necessary.**

B. Advantage: identifying the right target

Here, advantage means the ability to identify opportunities and to ascertain which of a range of options will produce the greatest benefit. It involves finding resources and having the vision to see ahead.

Again, here are some questions to help you think about this theme.

	Yes/ no/ maybe
● Have you had experience in spotting and selecting opportunities?	yes
● Do you think you may have an instinct or gift for it?	no
● Can you get the best out of a situation?	yes
● Are you able to pull in the resources or expertise you need to make the most of an opportunity?	yes
● Can you visualise a future successful outcome?	yes

For the social entrepreneur, advantage may mean having the judgement to select not only the right issue to address but the best way to respond to it from among several possible strategies. Advantage combined with focus makes a strong foundation for any entrepreneur, commercial or social.

So the questions were driving at a number of things:

- Picking the best opportunity from multiple possibilities is a key trait of the successful entrepreneur.
- An entrepreneur is the sort of person who can't help getting stuck in.

- Excessive analysis is unhelpful. Of course, you have to go into some detail before you can understand an opportunity's potential, but seeking too much factual reassurance can lead only to paralysis. Some decisions call for a leap of faith. Try not to get bogged down in over-evaluating things.
- If you don't like asking for help or aren't very good at it, your enterprise is likely to struggle.
- It's the vision of a better state of affairs that makes someone a social entrepreneur and provides them with the underlying motivation to persist.

So, do you agree with the following statement?

> **Yes, overall I feel I can see opportunities and make the most of them.**

C. Creativity: ideas, opportunities, solutions

According to Bolton and Thompson, entrepreneurs have lots of ideas and see opportunities all around them. They enjoy confronting a problem and coming up with solutions.

See how you score on the creativity front by answering these questions:

	Yes/ no/ maybe
● Are you an ideas person?	
● Do you understand the conditions in which you work most creatively?	Yes
● Do you enjoy solving problems?	
● Do you like encountering new situations, challenges and roles?	
● Are you comfortable sharing your ideas with others?	

Bolton and Thompson describe creativity as a 'servant' — it fuels the other facets of being an entrepreneur by providing the opportunities from which advantage selects and focus delivers.[11] Ideas alone are not enough — it's the ability to turn them into something real that counts.

The entrepreneurial character is strong on inventing the new, discovering something that can be turned to advantage or solving a challenge that leads to change. This is the opposite to preserving the status quo or leaving things as they are, whether it is a market for a product or an embedded social problem. If you don't feel the need to change something, you aren't going to be an entrepreneur.

The social entrepreneur needs to be creative in coming up with new solutions to old problems on which people may have abandoned hope about the possibility of progress, as well as effective solutions to new or urgent problems for which there is little time to waste. A solutions person is a precious commodity.

Ideas people need to pay close attention to their personal style: how do they come across to others whom they will need to persuade if their ideas are to be adopted? If they don't, would-be visionary leaders or creative forces run the risk of being typecast as mad inventors or frustrated fixated bores, according to creativity guru Anne Miller.[12]

Or you may be better at developing other people's ideas: for example, by franchising an existing scheme. This is a perfectly legitimate role for an entrepreneur or social entrepreneur. But it will help you to know whether you are strongest at coming up with original ideas or simply taking and adapting ideas from others.

Now that you have had chance to think about your creativity, do you agree with the following statement?

> **Yes, I have creative abilities that I can see might link to entrepreneurial activity.**

D. Ego: how you see yourself and others see you

We've covered the core entrepreneur features of focus, advantage and creativity; but Bolton and Thompson add two more: ego, which connects many of the general personality features to the specifically entrepreneurial ones, and team, which helps you know whether and how you work best with others.

In Gallup's analysis, 'ego drive' refers to 'wanting to make a recognised difference', while Bolton and Thompson use the term to refer to 'the inner self. . . what makes us tick and gives us purpose.'[13] They say a strong ego is crucial in making the most of your talents. Inwardly, this involves self-assurance, dedication and motivation; to the outside world, the notable characteristics are responsibility, accountability and courage. You want to be in charge of your destiny, make a difference, leave a legacy. You can face setbacks and overcome resistance. You are driven, a self-starter, confident and determined, probably competitive. You could be arrogant, even selfish, depending on where your sense of purpose comes from. The ego element enables the talents of focus, advantage, creativity and team work to be effective.

Ego is closely linked to the general personality traits we explored in the opening section, as the table below shows. Can you identify a potential entrepreneur within yourself, or see aspects you will need to work on?

Persistent		dedicated (Gallup), stubborn, determined, courageous
Optimistic		visionary, forward-looking, good visualiser, positive, ambitious
Proactive	...relates to...	activator (Gallup) or action-oriented, self-starter, initiator
Relational		networker, communicator, persuader, inspirer, encourager, wooer, winner-over of others

Other researchers have identified other traits such as the willingness to admit when you are wrong or to change direction; to work quietly or humbly; and to allow others to share the credit.[14] (This behaviour could take more self-confidence than thinking you are always right and deserve all the credit!)

Now think back to your answers in section 1 and how they would be applied in an entrepreneurial context. Do you agree with the following statement?

> **Yes, I feel I have the inner strength and outer resilience to underpin an entrepreneurial path.**

E. Team: better together or on your own?

Great entrepreneurs build good teams. The team facet, according to Bolton and Thompson, is about the ability to pick good people, to work through a team and to network. The Gallup themes also include 'expertise orientation' (knowing your own limits and finding experts to assist) and 'individualised perception' (the ability to see and use strengths in others). Not all entrepreneurs have this but, when they do, it multiplies what they can achieve, particularly in social enterprise where collaboration and partnership building are important.

Now reflect on these questions and consider what your response would be:

	Yes/ no/ maybe
● If you haven't had a chance to build a team in your life so far, would you be able to sense which people might be good to work with, identify their strengths and bring them into your team?	*a little*
● Do you enjoy getting out and meeting new people (networking)? (If you don't you will limit your success, as this is a key way to push forward new ideas.)	*yes, very*
● Are you happier and more effective working in a group, or do you feel more comfortable on your own?	*group*
● Do you recognise that you can't do everything by yourself and know when you need to bring in others to help?	*yes*

Finally, do you agree with the following statement?

> **Yes, I'd rather be part of a team and can imagine taking a lead in the right circumstances.**

3. What is the strength of your social motivation?

Our final cluster of features centres on the nature and strength of the social entrepreneur's social commitment. Bolton and Thompson regard the social dimension as one of the six facets that can turn a conventional entrepreneur into a social entrepreneur, and identify four components: belief, values, mission and service to others. The four elements build on one another: our beliefs on what life is about and how it should be will shape our values, which underpin the mission whose expression is service to others.[15]

You may already be involved in volunteering, charity work, making donations or contributing to corporate social responsibility programmes. Or you may simply have the desire to do something. These ten questions should help you assess the degree of social commitment you already have or might be able to develop.

What are these questions trying to uncover?

	Yes/ no/ maybe
1. I feel I can help make the world a better place.	
2. People are basically good.	
3. I get satisfaction from being involved in the community.	
4. I am motivated by a cause.	
5. I believe I have ethical values that I am able to live out.	
6. I find it hard to ignore suffering.	*yes*
7. I'm not fixated by money.	
8. I'd like to do more to solve problems and help people.	
9. I get angry when I see avoidable problems in the news.	
10. I can see how combining a social mission with entrepreneurial methods could multiply the impact.	

Q1 You want to make a difference to the world and believe you could in some way.

Q2 If you think people are basically bad you'll find it hard to sustain the motivation to help. Social entrepreneurs are invariably optimistic; how else could they strive towards a vision of a better future?

Q3 If you're not involved in the community in some way or don't enjoy it, your social facet is either undeveloped or a matter of principle rather than practice.

Q4 You have one or more social causes that really inspire you.

Q5 This question asks you to think about whether you are conscious of your own values, whether they are positive, and how far they guide your actions.

Q6 Your answer will show whether you feel social motivation or compassion, although you will need to be able to prioritise who you help and when to avoid losing focus. Do the needs around you spur you to action, or do daunting issues leave you discouraged and apathetic?

Q7 Money is vital and you will need to use it effectively, but if you are preoccupied by it you will probably not be happy as a social entrepreneur where the personal financial rewards are likely to be lower.

Q8 The important thing here is the desire to go further to develop your mission.

Q9 Properly channelled, anger can be a powerful motivator: if you aren't capable of getting angry you may lack the urgency and drive you need.

Q10 This is really the key insight of social entrepreneurship, as will be clear by the end of the book if it isn't already.

If these explanations have changed your view you may want to adjust your original assessment. If you answered positively on most of the ten questions you are definitely socially oriented. And if you can add this element to an emerging entrepreneurial profile, you have the potential to become a social entrepreneur if you aren't one already. Now see if you agree with the concluding statement.

> **Yes, I feel I have a sense of social commitment.**

Putting it all together

How did you get on with all these questions and themes? Do you have *some* of each of the qualities and attitudes?

What we are looking for is the combination of:

- The sort of person who likes a challenge or solving problems
- An entrepreneurial approach or potential (willingness to give it a try)
- Social motivation.

It's important to stress that a social entrepreneur is more than just an entrepreneur with high ethical standards or a socially minded entrepreneur. The social aspect is not just bolted on to the entrepreneur; the two are woven together. A social entrepreneur is a particular type of entrepreneur who makes entrepreneurial approaches the servant of social goals.

All the elements should ideally work together in a complementary way. You want to score high in each of them without going to extremes. The whole should be greater than the sum of the parts. Consider the power of connecting up the different areas:

- Add a creative or ideas-oriented personality to the entrepreneurial ability to sift and appraise ideas to uncover promising business opportunities
- Then add relational and networking aptitudes to persuade supporters and collaborators of the need to respond to an issue in a particular way
- Finally use relationship-building skills, strategic thinking, pragmatism and organisation to build a team to tackle the social problem.

If you feel you are weaker in particular areas, take heart:

- High social motivation can compensate for areas of weakness elsewhere.
- Good business skills can enable you to tackle a range of social projects.
- An infectious and positive personality can make others want to help you achieve your goals.
- Good teamwork can make up for many personal deficiencies.

It's not just a question of the aptitudes you already have: nature can be nurtured to some extent. Bolton and Thompson believe that 'Talent and temperament are the raw materials. By structured and unstructured learning and experience we can develop talent, manage temperament and impart technique to enhance and develop skills'.[16] Four of the six facets are predominantly based on innate talents, but they can still be improved:

- Focus can be improved by time management and project planning tools.
- Advantage can be enhanced by decision analysis and financial tools.
- Creativity can be drawn out through brainstorming and problem-solving exercises.[17]
- Team skills can be improved via leadership and motivational courses.

If, for instance, you feel you lack the confidence to throw yourself into a venture, it may be that you haven't yet had the 'Excalibur moment' described by Craig Dearden-Phillips: the experience that makes you believe, perhaps for the first time, that you must pick up the metaphoric sword and that it's meant for you personally.[18] It is this moment that can create the motivation for you to learn or to seek the resources you will need.

Have you had a dawning realisation about yourself? Are you already working hard in a creative way to bring about social change? Perhaps you are already a social entrepreneur without ever having thought about it. This is one of the reasons why the term needs to become better known so that existing social entrepreneurs can benefit from the self-knowledge and support networks that would open up to them. If you aren't yet a social entrepreneur, perhaps the term appeals to you in a way that makes you want to know more?

You may have done other psychological tests that confirm or modify your findings here. One of the most popular is the Myers Briggs Personality Type Indicator (MBTI). Here the classic formula for the entrepreneur is ESTP (although ENTP and ENTJ have been identified in some cases):[19]

E: extroverted rather than introverted
S: uses sense rather than intuition (N)
T: thinks rather than feels
P: perceives rather than judges (J).

We would expect the social entrepreneur to be close to this, but perhaps scoring an N for intuition rather than an S for sense and an F (feeling/friendly) rather than a T (thinking/tough): therefore an ENFP. If you are interested in looking at this further, you can do your own profile (various free versions are available on the web) and see how you come out.

Another test common in business circles is a Belbin Team Role Inventory. This looks at your characteristics and how you contribute to a team. In this analysis entrepreneurs can show up as 'plants,' 'shapers' and 'resource investigators.' For a would-be social entrepreneur, this test is most useful in helping you assess the people you may bring in alongside you. They should have characteristics that balance or mirror yours: if you are entrepreneurial, you will need an organiser to complement your drive and compensate for your likely weaknesses. This, more than the ability to pick technical skill sets, is at the heart of the team-building process.

Many entrepreneurs would prefer to go it alone, but recognise they can achieve more with the right team around them. Be honest about your temperament though: if you can't curb your independence or stop being a loner you will struggle to work in a team.

Another word of caution: if you are much stronger on the social facet than the others you may find business disciplines difficult and revert to a charitable mentality. You shouldn't duck the conflict between profit requirement and social need. A strong social motivation may dispose you to say yes to requests because you don't want to suffer the embarrassment or cause the upset that saying no might bring. This is an ego issue and you need to let your 'advantage' and 'focus' facets help you prioritise, which will mean being a bit more ruthless from time to time. Learning to say no without causing offence is part of the armoury of assertiveness skills, which can be learned through widely available training courses and materials.

Another possible role

If you feel after reading this chapter that you really don't have the characteristics to be a social entrepreneur, don't give up. There is a key place for what Bolton and Thompson call 'entrepreneur enablers': those who help support and develop others so that they can reach their full potential.[20] This applies equally to social entrepreneurs, who need encouragement and support in the challenges they face.

You may be better at helping others fulfil their potential than being entrepreneurial yourself. By putting your skills to work as a mentor or supporter of a social entrepreneur or as a member of the board of a social enterprise you will be playing an extremely valuable and worthwhile role.

Choices

You can make a number of choices about becoming or supporting a social entrepreneur. Consider your comfort levels: are you prepared to leave a job you could easily stay in to pursue an alternative career and perhaps take a lower salary? Letting your values dictate your actions may not be something that your career or upbringing has given you much freedom to do so far. Because social enterprises tend to be explicitly driven by values, they may give you the opportunity to align your work with your guiding principles.

Spend time reflecting on your values and whether you want to express them through a career based on causes. The dissatisfaction caused by work that conflicts with our values is unhealthy, so you'll be doing yourself a favour!

But I'm not trying to push you to be something you're not. Rather, I'm aiming to start you thinking in a new way about what you are, what you could be and what you want to be.

■ ■ ■

There is space in this book for only a brief overview of personality types and traits. For a fuller investigation into the dimensions of entrepreneurship, I recommend Bolton and Thompson's *The Entrepreneur in Focus: Achieve your potential*. It's also a good idea to sit down and talk things through to get a second opinion and advice on what to do. A local business adviser or social enterprise support group should be able to help you (see the appendix of resources for a starting point).

I hope that reading this chapter has led you to discover something new about yourself, or perhaps confirmed that your hunch about your social business potential was right. If you are strong on the social dimension and comfortable with most of the others, you have a good chance of being a social entrepreneur. If you are strong on all except the social aspect, you should probably go into business, if you aren't there already. (But try and give away lots of money and look for ways to make the world a better place.) If you don't feel you can be a social entrepreneur or an enabler, you can still be a supporter, funder or mentor.

By reading on you will equip yourself with a deeper understanding of what it means to get involved in social enterprise in some way. Who knows, when a life-changing cause confronts you, you may find you have the means to respond.

Pause for reflection and action

- Reflect on the outcomes of the self-analysis. Ask a friend whether they agree with your evaluation.
- Consider doing a second test (Myers Briggs or Belbin) to confirm your findings.
- Talk to a local social entrepreneur or support group such as UnLtd, Ashoka, the School for Social Entrepreneurs or Business Link (see appendix).
- See if you can find a taster course on social enterprise or social entrepreneurship (see appendix). It will quickly help you work out if this is for you.

4

Four leading social entrepreneurs

'The revolution — led by leaders committed to social entrepreneurship — is fundamentally changing the way society organizes itself and the way we approach social problems.'

D. K. Matai, Philanthropia

S ocial entrepreneurship is becoming a worldwide phenomenon. All the social entrepreneurs we'll meet in this chapter exhibit some of the characteristics we looked at in chapter 3. They have been selected because they aspire to take their ideas global, or have already done so.

Let's start with one of the best known and most successful social entre-preneurs, Muhammad Yunus, and find out how you get a Nobel Peace Prize for being a social entrepreneur.

The academic who took action

How much did it cost for a university economist to set up a completely new form of bank that everyone told him could not work? The answer is US$27.

In 1976 US$27 wasn't big money – little more than US$100 at today's prices. But that was all it took to set a whole village on its way to economic independence.

At the time, Yunus was a 36-year-old professor at the University of Chit-tagong in south-east Bangladesh. He had grown up in a family of modest means, the third of 14 children of whom five died in infancy. His goldsmith father always encouraged his sons to seek higher education, but Yunus's biggest influence was in fact his mother, Sofia Khatun, who always helped any poor person who knocked on her door. The young Muhammad did well at school and earned a scholarship to the US, where he experienced the protests against the Vietnam war and became an activist for Bangladeshi independence from Pakistan. He returned to the newly independent country to take up a university post.

Then, in 1974, famine struck. The sight of starving people coming to the city to beg shocked him and made him question his profession and moral values. He began to get involved in tackling rural poverty through irrigation projects. But it was a field trip to the poor village of Jobra not far from the university campus that burst his academic economist's bubble. Yunus and his students interviewed a woman who made bamboo stools, and learned that she had to borrow money before she could buy her raw materials. After repaying the middle man, sometimes at rates as high as 10% a week, she was left with a tiny profit margin. If she had been able to borrow at less exorbitant rates, she could have built an economic cushion to raise herself above subsistence level.

Yunus realised his cherished economic theories didn't fit the reality experienced by this woman, or by any of the basket weavers in the village. The market was 'sub-optimal' – it was failing. He approached a bank but it refused to lend the small amounts of money that these people needed. It objected that the poor are not reliable borrowers; that they have no collateral (security); and that it costs too much to administer a small loan.

So Yunus took matters into his own hands. He took the equivalent of US$27 from his own pocket and lent it to 42 basket weavers. With this tiny amount, he found it was possible not only to help people survive but to create the spark of initiative and enterprise they needed to pull themselves out of poverty. When the basket weavers repaid him he approached the bank again, but to no avail. Yet he knew the people concerned were good borrowers and that collateral was unnecessary. He felt that large numbers of small loans and repayments could be administered efficiently if the process was organised in a different way from that of the traditional banks.

Yunus gradually widened the geographical scope of the experiment to check it still worked without his close personal involvement, in case its previous success had been down to his personality or the sense of obligation people felt to him. He eventually persuaded a bank to put up its own money, but only by offering himself as a guarantor. He would have to pay up for any defaults.

By 1983 it was clear that the model worked. Although Yunus had secured sporadic support from banks and other funders, he took a big decision to set up an independent bank. He called it Grameen (or 'village') Bank. You can read the full story in his own book *Banker to the Poor*.[1]

By 2008, Grameen had grown to around 2,500 branches with 25,000 staff serving 7.5 million borrowers in 80,000 villages. On any working day it collects an average of US$2 million in weekly loan repayments. Of the borrowers, 97% are women and over 98% of the loans are paid back, a recovery rate higher than in conventional bank lending. According to the bank, 64% of borrowers' families have climbed above the poverty line.

Grameen's methods have now been applied in projects in 58 countries including the US, Canada, France, the Netherlands and Norway as well as developing countries. The charitable Grameen Foundation helps to spread the message more widely through support and development work, and has begun to operate even in countries that are difficult terrain for foreign non-governmental organisations, such as China.

From inspiration to institutionalisation

How did Yunus take the principles of the early individual loans and gradually institutionalise them without losing the personal touch and the qualities that made the project special? Ensuring that the bank remained true to its values while operating in a commercially viable manner was a huge achievement. The process was gradual:

> 'In creating Grameen Bank I never had a blueprint to follow. I moved one step at a time, always thinking this step will be my last step. But it was not. That one step led me to another step, a step which looked so interesting that it was difficult to walk away from. I faced this situation at every turn.'[2]

In fact, Yunus went further than simply adhering to his original principles by developing a series of innovative and effective programmes. Responding to criticism that the bank was only lending to the top layer of the poor, he introduced a 'struggling members' programme' for beggars. He saw the opportunity for many of them to sell small items such as sweets and toys as well as beg, and the bank advances modest interest-free loans to help them do this.

Other of Yunus's innovations included housing loans that proved highly popular and enabled 600,000 houses to be built; phone loans to 100,000 'telephone ladies' who now act as the hub of village communications by offering people access to mobiles without the expense of buying them; and a range of savings and pension products. Independence from external funding came when Grameen started to generate money internally by collecting deposits. Now Grameen has more money in deposits than it lends out to borrowers. This has helped people to save – crucial in a country that suffers regular environmental threats – and enabled rural communities to keep much of the money that used to leak away to the outside world.

How did he do it?

How did one man rewrite banking practice? His key insight was to replace collateral with trust, but not *blind* trust, which would have been open to abuse and therefore difficult to sustain. Yunus made two counter-intuitive innovations: lending almost exclusively to women and only in small groups or borrowing circles. He saw women as pivotal to domestic economic production and as more trustworthy than men when it came to repayment because of their concern for their children's welfare. In the rural Bangladesh of the 1970s this initiative met resistance from upholders of traditional Islamic views on the role of women and the charging of interest, but thanks to sensitive incremental work (such as looking for ways for women to work within the home so as not to offend cultural sensitivities) the model proved successful.

The borrowing circles consist of five women who support one another and provide a mutual guarantee if one should get into difficulties. The power of relationships has been harnessed to provide what the banking system can't offer: human cooperation. The ultra-high loan repayment rate proves that large numbers of people will do the right thing if they are given the right support and incentives. Repayment is a condition of further loans. But borrowers are called 'members,' not clients, as each borrower buys at least one share in the company – a crucial conceptual difference that makes interest more culturally acceptable.

Microcredit, as it is called, relies on the key insight that people of very limited means can be trusted to borrow and repay money under the right conditions. As Yunus puts it, 'It is not that the poor are not creditworthy, but that the banks are not people-worthy.' He observes that 'The poor always pay back.' The economist's insight was that you need a dollar before you can get the next dollar; all you need is someone to provide the first dollar. Yunus goes so far as to say that the right to credit is a basic human right. Although not a right that is commonly espoused, it will go a huge distance to tackling poverty.

The practices of Grameen Bank have had other far-reaching and often unexpected consequences. One has been the fostering of democracy: each borrowing group elects a chair and secretary, thus building up skills in leadership, decision making and civic participation. Grameen has encouraged its members to vote in local and national elections, where turnout has increased. More recently, Grameen members have begun to stand as electoral candidates to make a better country.

The housing loan scheme seems to have produced another benefit – a reduction in the national divorce rate – as a by-product. In keeping with Grameen's focus on women, its housing loans require the title deeds of a property to be transferred to the woman of the household. Cases of casual divorce where the husband takes the property and leaves his wife and children without assets are believed to have dropped as a result.

All the bank's profit (US$20 million in 2006) is transferred to a rehabilitation fund for disaster recovery. In a country so prone to tidal and wind damage, most recently the November 2007 cyclone that claimed tens of thousands of lives along the coast, this is an invaluable resource. And Yunus recently pointed out that Bangladesh has been reducing poverty by 2% a year since the turn of the millennium. If it is able to sustain this rate it will halve its number of poor people by 2015.[3]

The citation for Yunus's Nobel prize observed that 'Lasting peace cannot be achieved unless large population groups find ways to break out of poverty. Microcredit is one such means.' By building trust, elevating the role and status of women in society, and creating a basis for peace, Yunus has shown in a very practical way how to use financial capital to build social capital. Such is the currency of the social entrepreneur.

Characteristics of the social entrepreneur: lessons from Muhammad Yunus

If we take the facets of the social entrepreneur that we explored in the previous chapter, it's clear that Yunus has them all.

- Reflecting on the way he addressed each challenge, he says he felt 'I can solve it': a combination of *creativity* and *ego*, the motivation and inner confidence of the true social entrepreneur. Willing to take risk, he backed his own hunch and moved beyond his career comfort zone.
- His *advantage* facet found a way to achieve repayment rates the banks told him were impossible through a relentless focus on getting each new step right.
- In the way he listened to the needs of the poorest and built an institution that is still dynamic and responsive, he showed strong *team* qualities.
- A strong *social* motivation to transform the position of poor people in society enabled Yunus to challenge accepted ways of doing things – even those as apparently immutable as his country's banking system and cultural values.

The man with the word on the street

Our next social entrepreneur shares Muhammad Yunus's concern for marginalised people. In western societies over the past 30 years, the once rare sight of homeless beggars has become commonplace. It gave rise to one of Britain's (if not the world's) most visible expressions of social entrepreneurship: *The Big Issue* magazine. In city centres across the country, it can be hard to avoid – so much so that it has become the stuff of comedy:

Knock knock.
                    — Who's there?
Biggish.
                    — Biggish who?
No thanks!

                                        Peter Kay

The genius of *The Big Issue* is that it has created a simple, easily understood and widely acceptable response to homelessness. This is the genius of John Bird, who took the germ of an idea and made it a worldwide phenomenon. People are still approached by beggars every day in most sizeable cities the world over, but by buying *The Big Issue* you can be confident that your money will be doing good. Instead of providing a hand-out you are buying a product, and you know that there is a support system behind it that helps people with education and resettlement. Hence the slogan 'A hand up, not a hand-out.'[4]

Selling the magazine develops people's confidence and entrepreneurial skills. You may have heard some witty marketing banter from your local seller, and there is a system for pre-purchasing copies of the magazine that allows vendors to grow their own investment by selling a target number of copies. As vendors rather than beggars, homeless people become equal with the public, standing meeting your eye rather than sitting meekly to solicit your donations. The *Big Issue* salesperson has become an accepted part of the urban landscape.

Inside the UK edition of the magazine you invariably encounter John Bird, editor-in-chief and purveyor of opinions. He is an outspoken figure, a champion of the homeless, and a great social entrepreneur. What's more, he has made the magazine work as a business, exporting it to the US, Europe, South America and Africa. By 2007 there were 80 street papers in 29 countries.

Bird came from a poor background in west London, the third of six sons to a labourer father and barmaid mother. When he was seven the family was evicted for not paying the rent and the young Bird moved into a Roman Catholic orphanage with three of his brothers. His CV includes spells as a petty thief, homeless dropout and student at Chelsea School of Art, from which he was later expelled. By his twenties he had served several prison sentences for theft.[5]

Bird found stability and a sense of direction when he got involved in politics as a member of the Workers Revolutionary Party, became a printer, and ran a successful business. Then, at the age of 44, he approached a friend he had known since the 1960s, Gordon Roddick of the Body Shop, about publishing a book. Roddick agreed but had another idea for Bird: he had seen a street newssheet sold by the homeless in New York and thought it could work in Britain. Bird was sceptical, so he asked some homeless people what they thought. One replied: "Selling? Anything's better than begging."

The Big Issue was launched in London just a year later in September 1991, with the assistance of The Body Shop International. In June 1993 it went weekly, and regional sister titles were established in Manchester, Glasgow, Cardiff and Birmingham, followed by overseas editions in Sydney, Cape Town and Los Angeles. *The Big Issue* is a founder member of the International Network of Street Papers (INSP), which links up similar magazines from all over the world.

Vendors buy the magazine up front at the wholesale rate (40–50% of the cover price), sell their copies to the public and pocket the difference. This is a step on the way to earning a living. There are clear and simple rules governing the selling process, and the scheme operates other projects that help to resettle people and support them through health or addiction problems. All in all, *The Big Issue* helps between 8,000 and 10,000 people a year in Britain, of whom around 500 are active at any one time in London and 2,000 nationwide.

Bird says 'I measure our success on how many people we have stopped going to prison or having a premature appointment at the mortuary, how many people we have kept out of mental institutions or got out of loneliness, fecklessness, drink and drugs.' Research carried out among vendors found that 69% felt selling the magazine had boosted their self-confidence, 67% that it had increased their motivation to change things in their lives, and a third would turn to crime if they didn't sell the magazine. For nine out of ten vendors, it reduced the need to beg on the streets.[6]

As a person, John Bird is a habitual initiator: one of his schemes involves setting up an investment fund for social businesses. His attitude to creativity and risk is to keep starting new projects in order to discover which will succeed: 'You need to be able to fail and learn from it – to fail better next time.' His idea for The Bag Issue – a recyclable shopping bag with poetry on it – is one example that didn't see the light of day.

Bird's underlying philosophy is that 'I always try and explain that you have to be businesslike in whatever work you are doing. Even if it is giving services to the poor you have to think about delivery, levels of services, and the products you are selling.'[7] It is a principle that has shaped his journey from revolutionary politics to the social entrepreneur revolution.

Characteristics of the social entrepreneur: lessons from John Bird

- He is a *creative*, restless ideas person.
- He has adapted his business skills to a *social* challenge
- He has used *team* skills to form partnerships and work with influential people and gain access to the resources he needs. (However, his particular *focus* has earned him a reputation as a difficult person to work with in situations where hard decisions have to be made.)
- Personal setbacks can become a springboard for achievement (*advantage*).
- He didn't launch *The Big Issue* until he was 45. Social entrepreneurs don't need to start young; in fact, experience of the world is often valuable.

The doctor who lost patience with the drug companies

Now let's meet a social entrepreneur who is already having an impact on the health and livelihoods of millions of the world's poorest people, and could reach billions by taking the pharmaceutical industry in a new direction.

There is a Nigerian taxi driver – maybe working the streets of San Francisco at this very moment – who may be partly responsible for eradicating malaria and saving hundreds of millions of lives. Meeting him was the catalyst for Victoria Hale, a successful drug company scientist.

Years earlier she had dreamed of creating a not-for-profit drugs company to overcome the pharmaceutical industry's inability to convert promising treatments into commercially viable products that can be successfully sold in the developing world. But the business plan she drew up was so daunting that she set it aside. In January 2000 she found herself talking to a taxi driver about Africa's problems and her job. 'He said, "You guys make all the money." And then he laughed deep and heartily. His honest laughter was suddenly painful, like a knife in my soul. I took the exchange as a sign that it was time for me to try to realize my dream: to develop affordable medicines for neglected diseases.'[8]

Victoria Hale's parents had expected her to become a nurse. But as a child suffering from repeated ear and sinus infections she had experienced the relief that antibiotics brought and had decided to make medicines to help others. In her first job as a university cancer researcher, she felt the thrill of trialling new medicines that might provide a cure. With a PhD under her belt, she was well on the way to a glittering medical career in academia or industry. But she took the surprising step of moving to the US

Food and Drug Administration to satisfy her curiosity about the context of drug development. In 1995 she was offered a job in a private-sector pharma company that gave her the opportunity she had always wanted to make medicines.

A failing business model

Within three years, Hale found herself needing to take time out to think about the paradox that huge amounts of ingenuity go into developing new medicines, yet they frequently fail to reach the people who need them most. The pharmaceutical industry was dedicating less than 10% of its total research and development budget to diseases of the developing world, yet these diseases account for 90% of all infections (see box). Hale saw this as a fundamental problem: 'I wanted to find a way to separate business decisions from clinical decisions.'[9]

Treatable diseases of the poor

- Over 4 billion acute cases of diarrhoea occur every year, primarily in children in developing countries; 2 million children die annually from the disease.
- In 2002, almost 4 million people, many of them children under five, died of treatable lower respiratory infections such as pneumonia.
- Malaria infects at least 500 million people worldwide every year, of whom over a million die; 90% of cases occur in sub-Saharan Africa.
- Even though a cheap and effective vaccine is available, measles still kills an estimated 700,000 children every year.
- About a third of the world's population is infected with tuberculosis, which claims 2 million victims annually, 90 percent of them in developing countries.
- Almost 40 million people worldwide are infected with HIV/AIDS. New anti-viral drugs have turned what was a death sentence into a manageable disease, but in the world's hardest-hit countries, few patients have access to them.[10]

Pained at seeing dozens of potentially life-saving discoveries shelved for purely economic reasons, she asked a seemingly naive question. If lack of profitability is all that keeps these drugs from reaching the people who need them, why not take profitability out of the equation?

After that fateful taxi ride, she went to a drawer and pulled out the business plan for a not-for-profit drugs company that she had drawn up years before. With the active support of her husband, also a doctor, and funds from the consulting firm they had formed together, she founded the Institute for OneWorld Health (OWH).

The project was almost killed at birth by the tax authorities, which did not believe in the idea of a non-profit pharmaceutical company. And she had to overcome scepticism at the World Health Organisation (WHO): why would an American be interested in parasitical diseases?

A new business model

Drugs need to cost less than US$1 per treatment if poor people are to afford them. But at that price, drug companies can't recoup the US$100 million-plus they typically spend on development. So Hale set up a different funding structure. If a drug shows promise, she switches role from pharmaceutical researcher to broker and begins negotiating deals with patent holders, manufacturers, academics and funders.

Her new model is: unprofitable research leads + funding input + dedicated staff = viable drugs affordable by the poorest nations.

The first drug that she felt could be produced under this model was paromomycin, a treatment for black fever, the second most deadly parasitic disease after malaria. A visit to India's rural Bihar state underlined the urgency of what she was trying to do: 'I had never seen such poverty — people live on 30 cents a day — and many were dying a slow, painful and avoidable death from this disease.' Now being manufactured and distributed in India, the form of the antibiotic that OWH has developed could save up to 60,000 lives a year.

OWH is driven by a mission to tackle the inequitable state of global health. In rich countries, drugs and vaccines mean that infectious diseases now account for only one in 10 deaths. Yet among the poorest people in the world, as many as six in 10 still die of these diseases, according to WHO figures. Five out of these six deaths could be prevented if poorer people had access to the medication available in wealthier countries.

The economic cost – and benefit

The task is not just humanitarian, but economic. Illnesses prevalent among the poor disrupt communities and undermine a nation's economic growth. Such diseases as HIV/AIDS and tuberculosis strike young adults at a time when they would otherwise be contributing most to their family, their community and their country's economy. In countries where malaria and other comparable diseases are endemic, the scale of illness inhibits economic growth and discourages foreign investment. Africa's annual gross domestic product would be up to US$100 billion greater if malaria had been eliminated, according to the WHO.[11] The result is a vicious circle: the poorer a country is, the more difficult it is to eliminate disease, so treatable illnesses go unchecked and the nation's poverty deepens still further.

The good news is that OWH has identified a promising malaria drug that is now under development. Artemisinin justifies the label 'miracle drug': it's a three-day treatment that could save a million lives a year. But at US$1.50 per treatment cycle, the people who need it the most wouldn't be able to afford it. Hale's model tackles the shortfall: a major grant from the Gates Foundation is being used to create a cheaper large-scale replication process to close the financial gap and retrieve the drug from the commercial reject pile.

The drugs companies that donate intellectual property (patents, research and development, abandoned therapies) can enhance their role in global health and receive credit for their support. OWH forms partnerships with companies, non-profit hospitals and organisations in the developing world to undertake research into new cures and to manufacture and distribute new treatments that could transform the health of millions. In this way, Hale says, 'We challenge the assumption that pharmaceutical research and development is too expensive to create the new medicines that the developing world desperately needs.'[12]

An analysis in the *Stanford Review* identifies what it is that makes Victoria Hale a social entrepreneur:

> *First, Hale has identified a stable but unjust equilibrium in the pharmaceutical industry; second, she has seen and seized the opportunity to intervene, applying inspiration, creativity, direct action, and courage in launching a new venture to provide options for a disadvantaged population; and third, she is demonstrating fortitude in proving the potential of her model with an early success.*[13]

She has, they claim, mapped the contours of 'a new pharmaceutical paradigm' with the potential to achieve the same enduring social benefits apparent in the now firmly established microcredit industry. And just as Muhammad Yunus is recognised for building a basis for peace within a nation, it's conceivable that Hale's work might contribute to world peace by closing the health gap between nations.

Still only in her mid forties, this 'irrepressibly upbeat' woman clearly has the energy to pursue her ideas to fruition. She wears her array of awards lightly, but acknowledges the added clout they give her: a MacArthur fellowship arrived at just the right moment to drive home a deal; she won a social and economic innovation award from *The Economist* in 2005 and has been named Exec of the Year by *Esquire* magazine; she has a Pharmaceutical Achievements Award; and was declared Most Outstanding Social Entrepreneur of 2004 by the Schwab Foundation.

As one profile eulogises: 'Hale may not fit the stereotype of obsessed reformer, nor of economist, biochemist, or visionary executive. But she is, in fact, all of these things.'[14] The combination adds up to pure social entrepreneur.

Characteristics of the social entrepreneur: lessons from Victoria Hale

- Her childhood illnesses contributed to her motivation (social). She listened to her conscience when the taxi driver challenged her and was willing to change her whole career direction, despite the risks.
- She had the honesty and courage to ask searching questions about the status quo (ego).
- It took creativity to devise a new business model (advantage).
- She put her own money on the line and battled against obstacles and cynicism in the institutional environment (focus).
- Her corporate career stint was important: it meant she understood the pharma industry from the inside and confirmed her resolve to address its shortcomings (team).

The priest who protects the planet

There is one overarching theme that is capable of uniting or destroying us all, from Brazil to Bangladesh to Britain. It will determine whether any of the other initiatives we are considering will be anything more than fiddling while Rome burns.

What's the business model for saving the world? Here's a big vision: save the planet and while you're at it, create lots of work for people doing the jobs that are needed. Oh, and start with Australia.

Nic Frances is not your average Anglican priest. He is a serial social entrepreneur.

'I had been doing a range of things, including working in the hospitality industry and as a stockbroker. I thought it was all about making money. But at the same time, my heart was going, "Making money isn't enough." And the stockbroking really cleared up the dilemma for me, because it was just so much about making money that I realized I had to leave. So I moved to a poor area of Liverpool and I got involved in a whole bunch of things – I considered ordination as an Anglican priest, I started a drop-in for prostitutes, I taught in the local school. And one of the things I realized is that there were a lot of people that had old

stuff and a lot of people that needed it. So I started the Furniture Resource Centre, and for a few years we just picked up second-hand furniture and gave it away.'[15]

Just starting FRC was a socially entrepreneurial act, but it was arguably little more than a go-between charity. The real leap was to realise that the need for the service was perhaps a hundred times bigger than the 2,000 households being helped each year. This would be daunting for most people, but Nic Frances's view was 'There needs to be a market in this.'

With the backing of government, which stood to save money for every person who could be kept off the streets, 'suddenly we went from collecting second-hand furniture to building a business.' Turnover grew from a few hundred thousand pounds a year to around £5 million. 'We went from employing three people to 120 in two organizations – most of whom had been unemployed and homeless ... we had the experience every day of people bursting into tears as they received their brand-new furnished homes.'

Ten years later and the tears are flowing again, among the audience this time, as Frances addresses the inaugural Skoll World Forum on Social Entrepreneurship in Oxford in 2004. He describes the passionate commitment to people that drives his work, and the need to break down the barriers that stop us from expressing love for one another. He is honest enough to acknowledge that most of us, his former self included, turn a blind eye to the suffering and inequalities inflicted on others: 'I think the social entrepreneur is willing not to point at the problem but to recognize their part in it and join with others to take collective responsibility for changing it.'[16]

By this point, Frances had moved to Australia to head up the Brotherhood of St Laurence, one of Australia's largest charity organisations, with over A$25 million a year in philanthropic activities. It was a frustrating experience. He was a true social entrepreneur, buzzing with new ideas, but the organisation didn't know how to cope with them, or him.

Five years later, he had left and set up Easy Being Green (EBG), a commercial company providing resource-efficiency measures for private households. His goals for the venture were nothing if not ambitious. Knowing that some 70% of Australian homes change hands in any given ten-year period, he reckoned that if the government were to require the installation of energy-efficient lighting in any property being sold, most people would tolerate the cost (modest in the light of the broader cost of moving house) and appreciate the subsequent savings. This became the basis for EBG's campaign, and it began well with a deal with the state of New South Wales. As Frances put it, '70% of Australians in 10 years using 30%

less energy and water. That's a A$30 billion market. But we're not interested in the A$30 billion, we're interested in the 70% of houses using less, because then my kids are going to have an Australia that can be handed on.'

For Frances, though, Australia is only the beginning. 'I'm interested in a worldwide problem – global climate change – and I'm interested in a commercial solution because I think that's the only way you can have an impact on it.' His ambition is to run one of the largest businesses in the world, but a business driven by social and environmental objectives: 'Our goal is to change the planet.' But in the next breath, showing the entrepreneur's gift for communication, he brings the big idea home:

> 'If you see the size of the greenhouse gas pollution problem in America, it's huge. But imagine it instead as a problem shared by every single individual householder. If you see a solution that makes economic sense for each householder, as a government you can think to yourself, "Because it makes economic sense, all we've got to do is stimulate them into making that choice." And if the governments start thinking like that, I think we can actually start seeing real change.'[17]

The idea is not to force people to change against their will, regardless of finances or inclination, but to pull whichever levers – governmental, economic or self-interest – will achieve the most rapid change.

The leverage argument holds true for businesses too: they can build brand awareness and derive direct economic benefits from participating in the scheme rather than abstaining or objecting. Examples of France's strategic genius include striking a deal with ANZ Bank to offer free financing for Easy Being Green's fee with all new mortgages, and signing an ongoing agreement with Google in the US to provide green products and services to all its employees.

But to a pragmatist it doesn't matter which comes first: legislation to change behaviour or behaviour driving legislation. Frances is trying to tip people into mass consumer action – a cultural change. A key phrase for him is 'giving people the power to act.' And on the flip side, 'getting investors to understand the nuance of a social idea that pushes along a business opportunity.'

Such a mission is obviously fraught with challenges. People like Nic Frances provoke strong reactions, both positive and negative. For every business person in thrall to his paradigm-defining concepts, there is an environmental campaigner who regards the social entrepreneur's readiness to do deals as consorting with the enemy. These hard-liners see business as part of the problem, whereas Frances sees *not* doing business as part of the problem. In some ways life would be simpler if everyone maintained the old 'good guys versus bad guys' stand-off.

And once you are in the thick of the action, you make yourself vulnerable in other ways. When the New South Wales state government unexpectedly closed its carbon credits scheme, EBG lost a huge chunk of its work and income. If legislation or political parties change, the social entrepreneur who has built a business strategy on that platform can be left high and dry.

But Frances had already moved on. A restless, driven individual with a passion bordering on obsession, he sold his stake in EBG in order to set up a new company, Cool-nrg, to focus on cooling the globe through rapid large-scale energy-efficiency measures. Its first high-profile act was to secure a place in the *Guinness Book of Records* for the world's single biggest energy-efficiency undertaking: distributing 2.5 million low-energy light bulbs through a tabloid newspaper. Its sales also rocketed, a brilliant demonstration of how business and social goals can be aligned.[18]

In 2001, Frances was invited to be one of the first 30 Schwab Social Entrepreneurs, a group convened by World Economic Forum founder and chairman Klaus Schwab. At the 2007 forum focusing on market solutions to climate change, Frances was a star turn. His high profile opened up major opportunities to provide leadership for business, governments and communities to act on climate change and implement large-scale energy-efficiency programmes. In his new book *The End of Charity*, he uses this profile to lambast charities for perpetuating the status quo by failing to become more businesslike and engage in the market.[19]

Klaus Schwab describes Frances as a world leader in showing how social enterprise can set the global market agenda to address the world's biggest challenges. For all our sakes, we have to hope he succeeds.

Characteristics of the social entrepreneur: lessons from Nic Frances

- He is a highly *creative*, driven individual.
- He exudes a mix of self-confidence and vulnerability that seems to help him connect with his audience and communicate the urgency for change (*ego*).
- He thinks big: how far can an idea go (*focus*).
- He isn't afraid to try, accepting that things sometimes go wrong. When they do, he moves on to new things; those that work will keep going (*advantage*).

■ ■ ■

This chapter has looked at four prominent world-class social entrepreneurs. Though they come from different countries and backgrounds, they have more in common than sets them apart. Each shares the social entre-preneur's DNA: they operate by identifying problems that are so big they can be addressed only by systemic businesslike approaches. They see a vision of a new state of affairs, and look for the leverage point to achieve maximum disproportionate impact and cultural change. They show passion and compassion, turn necessity into opportunity, and pour all their ener-gies into seeing their strategy through.

Pause for reflection and action

■ Be a fantasy world-class social entrepreneur. Pick a social problem you think needs to be solved. If you could adopt any of the characteristics of our four case studies, what would you do to solve it?

5

Mega social entrepreneurs

'You've got to think about big things while you're doing small things, so that all the small things go in the right direction.'

Alvin Toffler, futurist

Imagine you are transported back in time to 1976, when Muhammad Yunus is starting out on the road to microcredit. You meet him just after he visits the village of Jobra and discover that he shelled out his own money to a bunch of destitute basket-weavers. What is your reaction?

Do you say 'That was kind, Dr Yunus,' but think 'Sucker! You'll never see that money again'? Do you exclaim 'You may have sowed the seeds for an entirely new banking system that will sweep the world! Have some of my money'? Do you hedge your bets with 'Interesting idea, nice if it works, I guess only time will tell'?

Or maybe you barely notice it or dismiss it as just a drop in the ocean of rural poverty?

Most of us, if we are honest, recognise that hindsight is a great gift. Sometimes we can spot potential, but it isn't easy to know whether or how it can be realised.

Anyone who wants to identify and nurture social entrepreneurship comes up against this problem. Could someone have spotted what Muhammad Yunus was doing, identified its potential and intervened to accelerate it? Could they have seen that Yunus had what it takes to go the whole way? At what point do you invest in an idea? Is it possible to design a reliable process for doing all of this?

If the answer to these questions seems doubtful, imagine the challenge of trying to set up a system to do this worldwide, with all the associated barriers of language and culture. Fortunately someone is already doing it. His name is Bill Drayton.

The social entrepreneurs' social entrepreneur

Bill Drayton was the first among a handful of visionaries to recognise the significance of social entrepreneurs to the wellbeing of their communities, and the strategic importance of supporting them in the right way to help them achieve their full potential. Although a social entrepreneur in his own right, he dedicates most of his efforts to supporting the growth of other social entrepreneurs to increase the impact of social entrepreneurship and bring greater coherence to the movement.

We might term such leaders 'mega social entrepreneurs' as they multiply the effect of their own skills and resources to achieve an exponentially greater impact. One person can only do so much, but they reach thousands, who go on to reach many more thousands if not millions – hence the mega impact.

To all intents and purposes, Bill Drayton has the air of a mild-mannered and modest professor. But his quiet force and determination belie the self-effacing image. Since 1981 Drayton has been steadily building an organisation that is transforming the way social entrepreneurs are discovered and nurtured and laying the foundation for a more professional, credible and systematic approach to the movement. It's called Ashoka (I'll explain why later).

If you are a social entrepreneur with the potential to deliver major change in your field or country, there is a good chance you will be contacted by someone from Ashoka offering you the chance to go through a selection process. If you succeed, you could be elected to a fellowship that gives you access to financial and networking support from peers who are among the top social entrepreneurs in the world.

Not had that call yet? Don't despair. There are only 2,000 fellows in the world so far.

To understand the significance of this movement we need to know more about the man behind it. Entrepreneurship came early to Drayton.[1] As a child, he took up crafts and established a shop from his bedroom, later producing a school magazine. His father was an explorer and archaeologist, his mother a professional musician. In his teenage years Drayton became fascinated by Gandhi's advocacy of non-violence as a means to social change, as well as his skill at political strategy and the marketing of ideas. Then he watched Martin Luther King adopt similar tactics in the US.

Unlike many social entrepreneurs, Drayton was an academic high-flier, first at Harvard University, then at Oxford, and finally at Yale Law School. Here he set up a project that connected law students with lawmakers to improve social policy. He was already being an entrepreneur, albeit an academic one.

His first proper job was in the 1970s, as a management consultant with McKinsey. Colleagues recall how he always aimed to solve things fundamentally by finding the point of leverage and seeking out the non-obvious solution. A good example came when he moved into public service in 1977 at the Environmental Protection Agency. The challenge here was to tackle industrial plant emissions, a task so complex and bureaucratic – governed as it was by hundreds of separate regulations for each process across all polluting industries – that it couldn't be implemented properly and was widely resented by operators. So Drayton set his entrepreneurial instincts and knowledge of human and organisational psychology to work and came up with a novel approach. The Bubble was a flexible incentive-based system that used financial mechanisms to secure better environmental outcomes. In other words, it was a way of getting the market to achieve public policy objectives, and it prepared the ground for the emissions-trading system that became the accepted standard for countering global warming after Kyoto in 1997.

Drayton knew intuitively that the way to achieve lasting change was to give people and companies a *reason* to do the right thing and to reward them. Ashoka biographer David Bornstein describes him as a 'bureaucratic entrepreneur.'[2] This seemingly paradoxical concept recognises that entrepreneurial methods can be applied to great effect in the most unlikely of contexts.

Ashoka: the world's first search organisation for social entrepreneurs

Meanwhile, Drayton was working with colleagues and friends to set up Ashoka. They made exploratory trips to India, Indonesia and Venezuela to see if they could figure out how to spot social entrepreneurs at an early stage and predict which of them would go on to have a big impact. They used networking to unearth people with a reputation for doing public good, especially those who were innovative.

Why the name, though? Ashoka was one of Drayton's heroes: a third-century BC Indian emperor who waged war to unite a huge swathe of southern Asia and then renounced violence and dedicated his empire to tolerance, prosperity and social welfare. Inspired by this reforming leader, Drayton had founded a society called Ashoka Table at Harvard. It brought students together with public and business figures to find out, off the record, how things really worked, so preparing the next generation to understand in order to lead. When he later came to set up his own international organisation, he felt the name was right as it was neither English nor made up.

Fittingly, the first Ashoka fellow was elected in India. At the first selection meeting in 1981, Gloria de Souza was chosen for her plan to revolutionise education. She was frustrated by the traditional approach to teaching in schools, which was based on outmoded colonial methods of learning by rote and in her eyes fuelled the ambition of many young people to emigrate when they were older. Her vision was to teach children to think for themselves, to be problem solvers and to create a new and better India.[3]

De Souza was not only a visionary teacher but a great marketeer, and her plans quickly gained support. Within seven years a million students were learning by her methods, and by the end of the 1980s the government had introduced them into the national curriculum. By providing critical support at an early stage to allow her to focus full time on the dissemination process instead of fitting it in around her day job, Ashoka enabled her dream to become a reality. The multiplication principle of the mega social entrepreneur was already in evidence. And how fitting that the first social entrepreneur Ashoka supported was herself devoted to helping others become problem solvers.

But the term 'social entrepreneur' hadn't yet emerged; nor had the funding to support Drayton's endeavours. Despite his high profile and eloquent advocacy, none of the big charitable funders would help. They just didn't get it, he recalls.

Part of the trouble was that there wasn't much to see. As a perfectionist, Drayton built his institution slowly and carefully. He knew he had to get the process right. But one early collaborator observed that he could make it seem as if he had an army behind him when all he really had was a couple of foot soldiers. All the same, he managed to convince early staff and funders that he had developed a methodology that would reliably winnow out the people with the potential to change society: 'the most valuable human resource that exists in the world.'

Panning for gold

Drayton describes social entrepreneurs as 'people who cannot come to rest until they have seen their vision become the new pattern society-wide.' They have 'the same personality type as entrepreneurs but applied in a different direction.'

As far as he is concerned, brilliance and conceptual ability are not necessary conditions, but a successful social entrepreneur does know their field inside out, can see what the historic next step is, and has the persistence and faith to get there. Drayton the analyst has built up a seemingly simple but profound method of selecting people who have what it takes (see box).

Ashoka's criteria for a social entrepreneur

Knockout test: is there a new idea?
   If so:

- **Creativity**. Two parts to this: is this person good at imagining the next step? And are they a problem solver? (What did they do at school? Did they show creativity there?)
- How strong is their **entrepreneurial quality**? Ashoka looks for people who can't rest until they have changed the whole of society. Is this person married to a vision? And do they get equally excited about how to achieve it? Are they pragmatic as well as idealistic?
- The **social impact** of the idea. Will it make a difference? Is it recognised as needed? How many people will it affect? How big are the benefits it will bring?
- **Ethical fibre**. Can this person be trusted? You can't lead if people don't trust you. The whole Ashoka community must be able to trust one another if they are to offer support, share ideas and grow. Trust is an intangible quality, so the selectors have to use intuition and gut instinct to nose it out.

In practice, the selection process begins with nominators in each country or region who are trained in what to look for and how to make strong nominations. An Ashoka rep then checks the nominees out. A second opinion is sought from another country to prevent emotional and cultural bias and to protect the local reps from undue pressure. (In some countries rejecting people is fraught with difficulty, so the reps can say the decision was not theirs – another illustration of Drayton's eye for the tiny detail that makes a big difference.) Then a jury of eminent social entrepreneurs, including one from another continent, decides whether to recommend the nominee to the global board for approval.

Cumbersome though this process might sound, Ashoka has learned that each step is necessary to ensure that the global board has the best chance of identifying a pattern-changing social entrepreneur. The strongest candidates make it through the process because of their passion; perhaps the rigour of the process prepares them for the challenges of becoming a full-time social entrepreneur. It is certainly designed to test them and their ideas over and over again.

You'd think that by the end of all this Ashoka would throw money at someone's idea. Not so. Early on Drayton decided that it would elect fellows – a rather quaint and academic approach, one might think. Each fellow is given a stipend of one to four years' pay at the public-sector rate for the area: enough to live on so that a fellow can leave their regular job to concentrate on the new project full time, but not so much that it promotes dependency or a lack of realism. Even more crucially, fellows get the support of other people who believe in them and their idea.

By the end of the selection process, a transformation often occurs. People who have been isolated and full of self-doubt are empowered to drive change without simply being able to 'buy' it. Clearly this is a carefully calibrated organisation designed to bring out the best in its people. The numbers speak for themselves: 71% of fellows have had their ideas adopted nationally or internationally.[4]

The first large-scale funder came on board in 1984, enabling Ashoka to work in Brazil as democracy returned. Along with many other countries emerging from dictatorships, Brazil started to open up to new ideas that responded to the need for social reform. Ashoka's early work here was spread across several fronts: education, health, agriculture, human rights (especially street children and indigenous communities), environment and housing. Today Ashoka has a wide funding base that includes the Skoll Foundation, and its annual income is in excess of US$3 million.

Pieces in a mosaic

The next stage of developing Ashoka was designed to multiply its impact still further: by examining how social entrepreneurs solved problems, Drayton hoped to identify common strategies and patterns. He developed a format for a 'mosaic' meeting in which scattered pieces – ideas – were arranged and rearranged in search of a picture in which they made sense.

At the first such meeting, in Asia in 1990, he found that several of the entrepreneurs had found a way of putting young people in charge of solving problems and making decisions in their projects. Principles such as this can be sifted and, if replicable, disseminated to others to speed up innovation: fifteen years later, for instance, Drayton set up his own organisation along these lines. Youth Venture rests on the belief that children are a great untapped resource in social change; used correctly, they have the power to 'flip' society very quickly. 'We would like to have every middle and high school become a place where there will be lots of examples of youth competence and confidence,' he says.[5]

Other high-level principles extracted from Ashoka's social entrepreneurs include:

- Having 'barefoot professionals' work in the poorest communities
- Designing new legal frameworks for environmental reform
- Helping small producers capture greater profits
- Linking economic development with environmental protection
- Unleashing resources in the community you are serving
- Linking the citizen, government and business sectors for comprehensive solutions.

The final stage of accelerating innovation is what Drayton calls 'blueprint copying' where trial and error can be taken out. Now the network is established it can multiply further via 'group social entrepreneurship,' mobilising ideas even more quickly.[6] Ashoka's E2 programme brings social and business entrepreneurs together to learn from one another, while its Global Academy promotes leadership through role models, looking to identify and support those who are changing history. Drayton seeks 'gigantic' and 'sustained' impact on six key themes: civic engagement, economic development, environment, health, human rights, and learning and education. Leaders of such projects include:

- Fazle Abed of BRAC in Bangladesh: bigger but less well known than Yunus's Grameen Bank, it covers all aspects of rural development.
- Peter Eigen of Transparency International, which tackles corruption at national or state level across the globe.
- Oded Grajew of the World Social Forum, set up as a counterbalance to the World Economic Forum.

People like this see the world as their agenda, according to Drayton. He believes that within five years, as the field comes together, they will be solving global problems through their combined networks and reach. Ashoka has deliberately chosen to focus on the top tier of social entrepreneurs so as to maximise the impact of limited resources and set a target to aim at. But Drayton's vision is not elitist: 'Everyone a changemaker.'

He believes that social entrepreneurs are at the cutting edge of historical transformation, and that the dynamic is unstoppable. 'This is one of those incredibly rare moments in history when there is deep profound change going on, and our job is to serve that. What a privilege.'[7]

What kind of person can create, sustain and go a long way to fulfil such a towering vision? Drayton's considerable abilities and experience span the public, private and third sectors. Without his background in economics and the law, and his love of history, he could never have built and maintained the organisation that became Ashoka: innovators for the public.

Characteristics of the social entrepreneur: lessons from Bill Drayton

These are qualities that Drayton not only possesses, but seeks in others through Ashoka's selection process.

- *Focus*: Drayton is focused to the point of obsession, fulfilling his own criterion of being restless until something is solved. He's also a perfectionist.
- *Advantage*: he saw something that no one else had seen, articulated it and began to make it a reality.
- *Creativity*: he found a way to nurture socially entrepreneurial talent across cultures without over-formalising the process.
- *Ego*: he subordinated himself to a greater purpose, but is stubborn enough to think he is right more often than not. He had to become good at delegating. He is frugal, too, not wanting to create a wasteful organisation.
- *Team*: he has built up a huge global network-based team. Despite inevitable frictions and differences of opinion, he is held in very high regard by those who have worked for him.
- *Social*: he is driven by an immense desire for the world to be better, and for people to fulfil their potential in addressing problems. He is an enabler of social entrepreneurship on a global scale.

Bill Drayton says of our second mega social entrepreneur: 'He is a business entrepreneur, he's a social entrepreneur, he is a role model. He's a person who has really strong values and he's demonstrating that.'[8] Who is he talking about?

A good story well told can truly make a difference[9]

What do you do if you have made your first billion by the age of 35 and can't see the point of making another? And what have eBay, a bunch of Oxford boffins and Al Gore's climate campaign got in common? The answer is Jeff Skoll, who became a social entrepreneur and applied his business brain to linking people up for social change.

We all know Skoll's business: eBay, the most successful survivor of the internet bubble of the late 1990s. But everything could have turned out very differently, since Skoll is a storyteller at heart and dreamed of being a novelist. He wanted to write books that would make a difference in the real world, warning people about problems and inspiring them to take action.

Earning a living got in the way, however, dictating a sensible degree in electrical engineering in Canada, where Skoll grew up. The idea was to find a platform for an entrepreneurial career that would make him enough money to free his time for writing. He started a consulting business and a computer rental firm. Then he realised he needed an MBA, so he took one at Stanford, where he met Pierre Omidyar, a man with an idea for an internet marketplace.

Skoll rejected the idea at first but soon realised its enormous potential. He joined eBay as its manager in 1996 and wrote the first business plan at the age of 31. He became eBay's president and first full-time employee, working crazy hours with Omidyar for two years without pay. Their business became the fastest-growing company of all time, growing from zero to US$2 billion in revenues in four years. It now has over 150 million customers worldwide.

Skoll Foundation

The foundation currently awards funding to 31 social entrepreneurs around the world to help them ramp up the scale of their projects. Eventually the portfolio will extend to 40 to 45 projects. Examples include:

Afghan Institute of Learning
Founded by Nobel Peace Prize nominee Sakena Yacoobi, the institute educates 350,000 women and children a year in Afghanistan and has trained 10,000 teachers.

Benetech
Founder Jim Fruchterman came up with the idea for a company that would develop and sell socially beneficial technology such as reading machines for the blind and low-cost land-mine detectors. 'My venture capitalist just barfed on the idea,' Fruchterman says. The markets were too small, and the big foundations thought his outfit sounded too much like a commercial company. But Skoll saw Benetech as a non-profit that could earn some revenue and maybe even break even, offering a high social yield for each non-profit dollar.

YouthBuild
After graduating from Harvard, Dorothy Stoneman joined the civil rights movement and lived in Harlem for 20 years. Seeing abandoned buildings, homeless people and idle youths moved her to start YouthBuild to create a better future for young people on low incomes. The scheme re-enrols them in its own alternative schools where they complete high school and build affordable homes for their neighbours while transforming their own lives. Each year YouthBuild engages 8,000 youths in local projects and produces housing for 1,000 poor or homeless families.[11]

Knowing what Skoll brought to eBay helps us understand what he has taken on in his current role. He brought together a community of people who can relate (usually successfully) online to buy and sell goods. This reflects Skoll's optimism about human nature: given the right incentives, he believes, most people would rather do good than bad.

When eBay went public in 1998, Skoll and Omidyar became overnight billionaires. Skoll stayed for another two years during which he established the eBay Foundation, endowed by the pair with shares prior to the public offering – itself an innovation that has since been much copied.

You might think that retiring at 36 with around US$5 billion in your back pocket is not designed to bring out the best in someone, but Skoll shuns the high life and has embarked on transforming the world of philanthropy in much the same way as he did the internet. He created and endowed the Skoll Foundation with US$600 million to combine the best of the business and not-for-profit spheres, supporting social entrepreneurs in tackling the world's biggest problems in a sustainable way. No less a business guru than Charles Handy observed that 'Social entrepreneurship is a natural blend of Jeff's own entrepreneurial instincts and his urgent desire to do something about the ills of the world by backing some of those working for social change and publicizing their stories.'[10]

Like Drayton's Ashoka, Skoll's foundation is seeking out and backing the changemakers, but in this case with an eye to providing organisations with appropriate secure funding. He looks for ideas capable of transforming a political, social or economic market and gives them three to six years of 'mezzanine capital' to help them achieve scale: go from local to regional, national or even international projects.

> 'The idea is that a little bit of good can turn into a whole lot of good when fuelled by the commitment of a social entrepreneur. We find the people with world-changing ideas, and then we empower them to effect even greater impact. . . . By connecting them to other change agents working around the world and by making their stories better known, we're participating in a global movement that shows enormous promise for the world.'[12]

So why is he doing all this?

> 'The world is a small and inter-connected place. We cannot ignore the plight of others in less fortunate communities or parts of the world ... many of the blights of the modern world (environmental destruction, crime, drugs, terrorism) emerge from the inequities between haves and have-nots.'[13]

As one of the haves, committed to using his fortune in the most socially productive manner possible, it is revealing that Skoll is prepared to identify inequality as the root of the world's gravest ills. And that he should choose to address it by focusing on social entrepreneurs: 'people who couple innovative ideas with extraordinary determination, tackling the world's toughest problems to make things better for us all.'

In 2003 Skoll endowed a centre at Oxford's Said Business School to study and nurture this kind of social entrepreneurship.[14] He chose Oxford because business schools in the US educate few foreign students, and he recognises that the movement has to be global. At the 2007 World Forum on Social Entrepreneurship there, he said:

> 'Today, wherever you find a social challenge at its worst, you'll find a social entrepreneur. We're witnessing a change in the nature of social change – from institutions to individuals and from governments to people.'

Like Drayton, he is fond of quoting Gandhi: 'A small body of determined spirits fired by an unquenchable faith in their mission can alter the course of history.'

Coming to a screen near you

Skoll now wants to use films to change the world. Finally in a position to give free rein to his storytelling side, and determined to find a way to reach more people with messages about the need for change, he founded his own film company, Participant Productions, in 2004. Its mission is social impact through social business: telling great stories that inspire change while building a new type of brand around social relevance in media.

Scripts have to show creative and commercial potential and raise awareness of one of six themes: the environment, health, human rights, institutional responsibility, peace and tolerance, or social and economic equity. If key partners in the public and third sector believe an effective awareness campaign can be built, the film gets the green light. Skoll's vision is to create an independent global media company focused on long-term benefit to society.

So the knockout test for every project is: how is this film going to make the world better? Participant believes that 'a good story well told can truly make a difference in how one sees the world. We seek to entertain our audiences first, then to invite them to participate in making a difference next.' Examples of films that made it to the light of day include *Fast Food Nation*, a dramatised version of Eric Schlosser's non-fiction book and a no-holds-barred exploration of the fast-food industry that reveals the dark side of the 'all-American meal,' and *An Inconvenient Truth*, the account of Al Gore's global crusade against climate change, for which Gore was awarded the 2007 Nobel Peace Prize.

It seems everything Skoll touches turns to gold: backing someone who ended up winning a Nobel prize was a smart move. And the campaign Gore ran alongside the film eloquently embodies Skoll's principle for Participant films; indeed, it even (self-referentially) features in the movie itself, as a tutorial on how to spread the message. You could tell Skoll was excited about it: 'This Al Gore film, whoa – this movie may save the planet. That's pretty cool.'[15]

Sceptics should note that these are far from being a rich man's vanity projects or worthy but dull films that fail to reach an audience. In 2005 Participant received 11 Academy Award nominations for *North Country*, *Syriana*, *Murderball* and *Good Night and Good Luck*. And these films are profitable: they have commercial discipline, the mark of the businessman as social entrepreneur. Participant has been described as a 'pro-social business' whose idealism is fundamental to its success.

In 2005, Skoll launched the Gandhi Project in partnership with Silicon Valley entrepreneur Kamran Elahian. Working with Palestinian actors, an award-winning director dubbed the epic film into Arabic. It is being screened throughout Palestine with a view to advancing civil goals of peaceful resistance, self-reliance, economic development and local empowerment. Plans are under way to extend screenings throughout the Arab world. Skoll shares Bill Drayton's optimism that personal action can precipitate global change: 'Not everyone can be Gandhi but each of us has the power to make sure our own lives count – and it's those millions of lives that will ultimately build a better world.'[16]

Influenced by the film experience, staff at the Skoll Foundation are now looking at potential social entrepreneurs with a view to the narratives and storylines that might inspire people to bring about social change. Films are being made to celebrate and promote the social entrepreneurs themselves. Expansion into other media and new opportunities for activism are at the planning stage.

Skoll has his eyes on the big picture, and on all the synergies. Entertainment and campaigning; entrepreneurship and change; no-profit, break-even and full-profit. His capital investments are steered by the same principles: they go into green energy, micro-finance and progressive firms. The underlying belief is that things that do good will become more valuable over time.

So Jeff Skoll finally got to tell his stories of hope and a better world. He just hasn't written that novel yet. But lots of people are writing about him.

Jeff Skoll: Q&A

Why did you become a social entrepreneur?
When I was young, I used to read a lot and it seemed that many of the trends in the world were scary: overpopulation, new weapons, new diseases, unsustainable use of the environment and other frightening things. My dream was to be a writer so that I could tell stories that would get people interested in the major problems that affect us all. My thought was that people are basically good and if you give them the opportunity to do the right thing, they usually do it. After all, we are all in it together, aren't we? My goal was to reach a point of financial independence as quickly as I could so that I could write these stories. I tried a few entrepreneurial ventures and then eBay came along. With the resources from eBay, I was able to create Participant Productions, my media company that produces entertainment to inspire and compel social change.

Along the way, after eBay had gone public, I met with John Gardner. John was in his late 80s at the time and had been the Minister of Health, Education and Welfare under Lyndon Johnson. He was the force behind the Great Society programs of the 60s. I asked him what gave him the greatest hope for humanity to survive into the future and he said 'good people doing good things.' I asked what I could do personally and he said 'bet on good people doing good things.' That became the inspiration for the Skoll Foundation.

I think I realised I was a social entrepreneur once I had started the Skoll Foundation and Participant. After I left eBay, I resigned my for-profit board positions and started dedicating all my time to work on the major social problems in the world.

What are the most important features of a social entrepreneur?
I believe that social entrepreneurs fill an important void in the world. For all the good that government, business, religious organisations and other institutions do, there are many problems that fall between the cracks – health, environment, human rights, poverty – and that's where social entrepreneurs come in. I believe, as John Gardner did, that social entrepreneurs are 'good people doing good things' and that they are the best hope for mankind to survive.

What advice would you give to business people, young people and politicians?
For business people, doing well and doing good go hand in hand, in my experience. When eBay went public we also created the eBay Foundation, and people were as proud about the latter as they were about the former. Businesses that support social causes gain happier employees and more loyal customers, and the more support there is, the better it goes.

As for politicians, I believe that movements need to start at the grass roots and that the politics will follow. That said, enlightened political leaders can help social causes considerably because of the massive resources they can deploy. Political leaders need to think about the next generations and not just the next election, and that is why it is so important to mobilise opinion at the grassroots level first before trying to mobilise political support.

contd.

For young people who are studying or have just finished school, the world is theirs to inherit. There are so many distractions it's hard to decide what to do with their time and professional careers. When I was in high school, I had a great teacher who made us do an exercise: write what you want written on your tombstone and then work your way backwards. For me that was a powerful motivation for all that I have done in my life so far.

Global economic giants embrace social entrepreneurs

Speaking at a press conference about the first social entrepreneurs selected by the Schwab Foundation, Muhammad Yunus said 'If I were a venture capitalist, I would provide funding for each one of these entrepreneurs. If I were a Hollywood producer, I would make a film to tell each one of their stories.'[17]

Klaus Schwab is a German-Swiss professor of economics who knows just about every world political and business leader personally. He is the founder of the World Economic Forum, the highly influential annual summit at Davos. And the good news is that he is passionate about social entrepreneurship.

Despite working among the elite since founding the forum in 1971, Schwab has retained a passion for alternative approaches. In 1998, he and his wife Hilde created the Schwab Foundation for Social Entrepreneurship in Geneva to support the work of social entrepreneurs. Their original idea was to make a huge splash with an annual US$1 million award to the top social entrepreneur. Procedures were devised to search out and judge the candidates, and a call went out for referrals and applications.

However, it rapidly became clear that singling out one person for the award would be a major challenge and raise some awkward issues. When the shortlist of 41 social entrepreneurs gathered at the 2002 World Economic Forum with the winner still to be chosen, the project reached crisis point. The Schwabs and their advisers realised that it would be wrong to select one winner, so they decided instead to honour each of the 41 equally and create a fellowship.

Klaus Schwab explains, 'I want to find people who have discovered practical solutions to social problems at the local level, solutions that have been shown to work to improve people's lives and that can be adapted to solve similar problems all around the world. I want to create a way to disseminate their accomplishments so others can support them or emulate their approaches.'

His wife Hilde elaborates, 'I'd like to see it become a real movement; I want young people to become social entrepreneurs.'[18]

It is clear the couple – a true partnership – are converts. Klaus says, 'The world must become aware of the fantastic transformational power of social entrepreneurship and the Foundation will work as a catalyst in this effort.' He is aware that globalisation has its critics and that it produces losers as well as winners, and his mission is to help social entrepreneurs and others to work together to mitigate its negative impact and find ways to do global business better. Describing social entrepreneurship as 'one of the new para-digms of societal development today,' he places it alongside public-private partnerships, social networks and global corporate citizenship as 'the new pillars that will form our society of tomorrow.'

Klaus Schwab's role in the World Economic Forum gives him an ideal platform to connect social entrepreneurs with business leaders: 'We in the Foundation are strategically placed to assume a brokering role, strength-ening the business-social bridge. We want to use our leverage to attract the notice of governments and business people so that the scalable solutions of social entrepreneurs can be replicated, improved and expanded, so that their practical insights can be incorporated into government policy and business initiatives.'

The different organisations we have reviewed in this chapter often have overlapping roles. Ashoka has picked up some social entrepreneurs in the early stages of their work, and Skoll or Schwab have funded their later expansion. Skoll has funded Ashoka to develop its work in general. A healthy respect and co-operation seems to have developed between the different organisations.

■ ■ ■

As we can see from the stories of these global players and organisations, in-fluential strategic thinkers are increasingly recognising that social entrepre-neurs have a central role to play in creating a better world. The mega social entrepreneurs featured here are hugely ambitious and determined to achieve major change. To do this they apply their business nous to maximise lever-age, seeking the most effective financial and political routes to make an impact. As a result, they are starting to influence governments and corpo-rations to put their own weight behind the social entrepreneur movement.

Encouragingly, the number of high-level foundations and strategic supporters of social entrepreneurship is proliferating: others include Omidyar Foundation, Echoing Green and UnLtd. Most of these organisa-tions have charismatic and socially entrepreneurial founders and drivers who seek to multiply their own personal impact through the social entre-preneurs they select and support.

Pause for reflection and action

- Browse the Ashoka, Skoll or Schwab sites to find inspiration (see the appendix at the end of the book for details) and to get an idea of where and in what fields their social entrepreneurs are active.
- Consider making contact with one of the social entrepreneurs or projects supported by the organisations above to learn about them.

6

Extraordinary ordinary people: Social entrepreneurs around the world

'I see myself as something of an accidental entrepreneur – made more than born. I happened on entrepreneurship through my social passion, not the other way round. And at no stage did anyone view me as remotely entrepreneurial as I was growing up – neither driven nor a consummate networker. All these traits followed the development of my social mission.'

Craig Dearden-Phillips,
CEO, Speaking Up

Once you know what you are looking for, you can see them everywhere. All over the world, social entrepreneurs are emerging. In this chapter we look at the sheer range and diversity of their activities around the globe.

Let's start by looking at the reach of the mega social entrepreneurs we've just met. Ashoka is active in 60 countries; Skoll and Schwab both work in more than 40. And there are of course various other foundations supporting social entrepreneurs and many social entrepreneurs themselves working away without full public recognition.

Ashoka's operations tend to be concentrated in countries where it has been active for some time: Brazil, Mexico, India, Indonesia. Even so, there is still plenty of scope for growth: Brazil, for example, has a population of 188 million and not much more than one major social entrepreneur per million people. In Africa, South Africa has the greatest representation, perhaps because of the accessibility of its language and culture, but Nigeria is not too far behind. Eastern Europe has seen an explosion of social intervention following the end of communist rule. The US is a hotbed of activity, tackling its own issues as well as exporting social entrepreneurs around the world. And partly for reasons of geographical proximity, Central and South America are strongly represented.

	Ashoka	Schwab	Skoll
Brazil	230	10	2
India	224	11	4
Mexico	121	5	
Indonesia	91	1	
South Africa	74	2	1
Thailand	71	1	
USA	70	17	17
Poland	59	2	
Nigeria	57	2	
Bangladesh	53	4	
Colombia	43	4	2
Nepal	35	1	1
Peru	29	2	1
Ecuador	26	1	
Pakistan	25	2	2
Egypt	20	2	
Turkey	18		
Uganda	13		
Venezuela	13		
Zimbabwe	11		
Sri Lanka	9		
El Salvador	6		
France	4	1	
Japan		2	
China		1	
UK		3	1
Kenya		1	2
Switzerland	1	2	
Palestine	1		
Latvia	1		
Total*	1,800+	104	38

* Figures for 2006/7. Includes numbers from other countries not listed in table.

National breakdown of numbers of social entrepreneurs supported by the three major foundations

Bringing up the rear are places where the need is less acute or there are cultural or political barriers impeding the development of the necessary infrastructure: Palestine, China, Japan, and parts of Europe.

Flushed with success

One thing you need wherever you are is decent toilets. If Jack Sim from Singapore has his way, his World Toilet Organisation will get to be just as well known as that other WTO, the World Trade Organisation. Sim has been lauded as a 'toilet technocrat, diplomat and acrobat all rolled into one flushing phenomenon.'[1] A successful construction entrepreneur, he became acutely aware of the public health and social problems created by the taboos surrounding a basic human function: excretion.

More than half of the developing world's population have no access to decent toilets. In India and China alone, a billion people without sanitary facilities relieve themselves on streets and in rivers, heavily polluting the water. The most serious source of water contamination in developing countries is human waste. Even when public toilets are available, they are poorly maintained. According to the United Nations, more than 5 million children die every year from sanitation-related diseases such as diarrhoea.

When I asked Jack Sim what drives him, he explains, 'I was born in 1957. Singapore was a poor country at that time. I lived in a village with a bucket sewage collection system. I've seen the full journey of Singapore from poverty to a first-world country with state-of-the-art sanitation and water treatment. If Singapore can manage it, everywhere else can too. We just have to act and make it happen.'

After starting Singapore's Restroom Association in 1998, Sim undertook three years of research and travel to meet groups in other countries, which he funded out of his own pocket. He launched the World Toilet Organization in 2001 at the first World Toilet Summit in Singapore. It was set up to focus on what people around the world are doing to improve the public sanitation infrastructure and to showcase their accomplishments so that others can learn from them.

With just US$250,000 a year, Sim has been able to organise five World Summits that have brought together around 400 participants from 25 countries. He has engaged governments and corporations alike in competing for the privilege of having the country with the cleanest public toilets. He has devised the Happy Toilet star-rating programme in Singapore, which rewards public toilets that meet stringent design, quality and maintenance criteria. The UK has its own variant, the Loo of the Year Award, and similar initiatives are being launched elsewhere.

WTO is a free and growing service: its 46 members from 36 countries pay no membership fees because Sim believes this would limit the organisation's growth and create unrealistic expectations. To compensate for its lack of financial resources, WTO's fundamental strategy is to use leverage.

Governments or corporations sponsor events because of the benefits they accrue. The organisation operates at several different levels:

- Setting standards and incorporating proper sanitation into public policy on environmental health, planning and building standards. The goal is eventually to develop global benchmarks for public toilets in city planning.
- Engaging businesses through market opportunities: WTO's awards are highly prized.
- Improving knowledge and training in ecological and sustainable sanitation by spearheading the World Toilet College to train people on site, on campus and online. Working with the Singapore Polytechnic, it offers courses in toilet architecture design, specialist restroom cleaning and ecological sanitation.

Business opportunities

Restrooms and the related infrastructure account for about 7% of total construction costs and thus constitute an industry worth tens of billions of dollars a year. Beijing alone spent US$100 million to create about 3,700 world-class toilets for the 2008 Olympic Games. WTO supports the creation of a star-rating system for lavatories in Beijing, and China reports it will also build millions of low-cost toilets in rural areas over the coming decades. Substantial investments are also being made in sewage plants and environmentally friendly technologies such as infrared sensors that save water and energy. As the saying goes, where there's muck, there's brass – profits are there for the making in clean toilets.

Humanitarian and health benefits

WTO mobilised its membership of international sanitation experts to partner Habitat for Humanity – an international non-governmental organisation that builds housing for the poor in developing countries – in helping to rebuild areas in Sri Lanka devastated by the 2004 tsunami. The new homes they build have a new feature: a toilet. Previously, most families used crude hole-in-the-ground toilets that often contaminated the groundwater from which their villages drew drinking supplies. Not surprisingly, incidents of diarrhoea were high, especially among children.

Other initiatives include tackling the toilet taboo in some cultures through education and direct unashamed action and raising toilet ratios for women, who tend to suffer from longer queues and inadequate provision. WTO sees itself as a global body championing more and better toilet environments and seeking to overcome the fragmentation of disparate agencies around the world.

This is not a niche that everyone would spot. If you were asked what you could do to save lives, show respect for women, tackle cultural taboos and capture a business opportunity, it's unlikely that the first thing that came to your mind would have been toilets. But social entrepreneur Jack Sim saw the possibilities and has built a successful strategy to exploit them.

Jack Sim: Q&A

What are your strongest entrepreneurial characteristics?
I'm a dreamer, and believe that dreams always come true. I'm a leverage strategist who aligns diverse interests into a common mission. I have a sense of urgency: life is finite and it's important to use it meaningfully. And I have a trusting nature that allows stakeholders to be empowered rapidly.

Why are you a social entrepreneur?
I believe it is all about using an entrepreneurial approach to create a social dividend. My 25 years of business experience come in very handy.

What are the most important features of a social entrepreneur?
To focus on the end customer, the poor, and not on self-justification, ego, status or self. True leaders must live and die for the cause. They must be confident, not fearful, doubting, or too emotional. They should be able to send out love to all, and to love and accept themselves with humility. Above all, stay focused on the mission.

Still waters run deep

For anyone who feels they might not be qualified to become a social entrepreneur, take heart. Reed Paget is a young American journalist who decided he wanted to set up a social business. The trouble was,

> 'I didn't know what a financial model was, a profit and loss statement, a balance sheet, a cash flow statement, I'd never read a business plan, I didn't really know the difference between marketing and advertising, I didn't know anything about sales, price, margin, bottle cap closures or pallet configurations.'[2]

But Paget didn't let his lack of business experience stop him setting up an exciting social venture that might just change the world. The business is belu, a bottled spring water. Profits from the operation are dedicated to funding clean water projects in the developing world and waterway cleansing in the UK.[3]

Reed Paget is a journalist and film maker with a passion for the environment. His moment of recognition came when he realised he could switch from sitting on the sidelines and pointing the finger to running his own company from an environmentally minded point of view. He could improve the environment simply by winning market share.

The marketing genius of his idea was to use a bottled water product to tackle the lack of clean water suffered by a quarter of the world's population. Here would be a consumer product that raised awareness while generating cash. Paget recognised that social enterprise can do more than highlight development issues – it can be a powerful way to influence big retailers and their supply chains.[4] To complete the picture, belu also seeks to minimise its waste and energy impact through carbon offsetting and by introducing biodegradable corn-starch bottles.

Paget's experience demonstrates the power of goodwill: many people helped make his vision a reality against the grain of normal business experience simply because they believed in his vision, cause and passion. That passion extends to volunteers, who have been hitting the summer festival trail along with staff to reach young people and future opinion-formers interested in ethical consumption. By reaching these early adopters and trendsetters, belu can start to spread product recommendations virally, so reaching consumers much more quickly than most high-budget advertising campaigns do.

Commercial innovation specialists '!What If?' have provided free consultancy input, reasoning that they can give to as well as take from cutting-edge social enterprises. They observe that belu's leaders' willingness to share the credit means top companies have been willing to come alongside and help them.

This cooperation has been important in belu's decision to professionalise in order to scale up, and to bring in a management team with the skills they need. This is a defining moment for many founder-driven social enterprises that seek to make the transition from relying purely on confident idealists selling a vision and covering all the bases themselves. Belu's participation in a social enterprise incubator at Community Action Network in south London is helping to accelerate its development through the network's specialised contacts and support networks.

Just as Paget felt he didn't know the things he should know when he started his enterprise, he has now recognised that his personal limitations were holding back his company's expansion. Clearly he knows more than he lets on, but in a way, what he didn't know has served him well, allowing him and belu to discover a whole new business model. If he had known just a little more, he might have talked himself out of even starting ...

Reed Paget: Q&A

What are your strongest entrepreneurial characteristics?
I'm driven by the big idea. In the case of belu it was launching a brand to address what I believe to be extremely important problems with water around the world. The idea of launching a compostable bottle made from corn and becoming the first carbon-neutral bottled water brand also inspired me. All of these things took an enormous amount of effort to achieve, but because they were inspiring for me and the rest of the team, it didn't feel like work so much as an exciting challenge.

The successes we have had thus far I would chalk up to another character-istic: looking at the top of the mountain (success) and ignoring the many crevasses (risks of failure) along the way. It may seem naïve, but it's only by being optimistic that we have come this far. Another way of looking at it would be the power of positive thinking.

It would be a rare person that has all the necessary business skills to make an enterprise run, but that's what a team is for, to ensure all aspects of the business are covered.

Why are you a social entrepreneur?
I've never considered that I am one. I do however feel there are issues with the world that need addressing and I see great scope for harnessing business to help provide solutions.

What are the most important features of a social entrepreneur?
Hustle!

Slums fit to live in

When Ashoka selected Somsook Boonyabancha as one of its first Thai social entrepreneurs in 1991, it was because it felt she had found a way to end the damaging deadlock that afflicts so many cities in the developing world: that between poor slum squatters on the one hand and the owners and devel-opers of the land on the other. She seemed to have what it takes to keep going and find solutions to seemingly intractable problems. Yet despite her considerable success, she remains a modest, self-effacing person who is reluctant even to be profiled, protesting that 'It's not about heroes.'

Boonyabancha has developed a methodology for land-sharing: an inno-vation in urban land use built around a mutually beneficial deal between urban squatters and land owners who wish to develop their property for commercial purposes. Everyone wins. The slum dwellers get new and better (if denser) housing on a back portion of the disputed plot at an agreed affordable cost, and become legal and secure in their tenancy.

Thanks to the orchestration of the deals, they also emerge better organised and more able to negotiate and deal with other problems in their lives. The land owners get their street frontage freed up for immediate development.

The term that Somsook Boonyabancha uses to describe her approach is 'people-centred slum upgrading.' It is a remarkable combination of psychology, law, town planning, creative architecture and property development. But how does it make her a social entrepreneur?

First, she is using innovative thinking to address an entrenched problem and seeking a lasting solution rooted in a win-win deal. She recognises that only by promoting a satisfactory outcome for both sides can she reach a sustainable outcome. She sets out to achieve this by balancing financial with social needs.

In everything she says and does, what shines through is not dry abstract theory but a passionate vision. Boonyabancha knows that the solutions to complex human problems can come only from the people concerned, not as isolated individuals but as communities working together. In one of her projects, landlord and former slum dwellers ended up as friends.

Second, Boonyabancha has a way of redefining problems so that solutions become possible. She sees slums not as 'an aberration, but a normal part of existing city structures.' Instead of being something to fear, they are something that can be improved. This insight is as important for those in power – the government, the landowners, city officials – as it is for the slum dwellers themselves, prone to descend into a self-fulfilling spiral of low self-esteem and lack of motivation for change.

The redefinition of problems goes further still. Boonyabancha looks for the positive elements even within deep poverty, particularly the creativity and commitment that can be unleashed when poor people are empowered to organise in pursuit of a better life:

> 'People carrying on their lives individually have no great power, they are practically invisible. But when people come together as a group, they are like a giant! If you have 150 families in a community and get them to work together very strongly, that group will become very visible ... This is the way to take care of people by people.'[5]

In statements like this one, she seems to be pioneering a new way of seeing the nature of a social challenge.

Project after project is proving that there is a way to break out of the trap of failure and turn a vicious circle into a virtuous one. Boonyabancha envisages 'a kind of university' emerging as poor urban groups become more aware of one another and ask *why* their situation is the way it is when they see others changing things. (Asking why is one of the hallmarks of the social entrepreneur, as we shall see in chapter 8.)

Money has a place in all this, of course. These programmes are costly. But the social entrepreneur is adept at leverage, Boonyabancha's third strength. As a member of the Thai government's housing ministry, she learnt how the system operates. Setting up an independent public organisation, CODI, in 2000 enabled her to operate with a foot in both camps, enjoying government funding but also a degree of freedom from government and access to other sources of income.

Over time she has been able to develop an impressive degree of leverage: influence over a funding stream worth US$ 240 million and an ambitious programme to reach 300,000 people in 200 communities over five years. She has perfected the art of weaving government and community agendas together to the satisfaction of both constituencies, acting as a social entrepreneur in the public sector.

An interesting aspect of her attention to leverage is the way the finance for upgrading has been structured. Not for her the heavyweight infrastructure costs incurred in some countries, to often disappointing effect, but more of a microfinance approach, where modest loans match the recipients' initially modest capacity to improve. Upgraders put in 'sweat equity' as they build their own homes and are able to draw on savings and loan products too so that they can develop their livelihood. The process is a holistic one.

Boonyabancha's ambitions extend beyond Thailand to a wider Asian audience, addressing challenges in Korea, Hong Kong and Vietnam. And like any pattern-changing social entrepreneur, she has found a way to standardise and replicate her principles so that they can be used over and over again in similar situations anywhere, even without her personal presence. It may take one person to come up with a breakthrough, but if they have to be personally involved every time their ideas are put into practice, their innovation will never take off.

What Somsook Boonyabancha is doing goes beyond traditional community development; it is socially entrepreneurial community development.

Earthly paradise

Tim Smit would hardly be an obvious candidate to regenerate a neglected and deprived part of Britain. This Dutch former pop musician abandoned the industry in his 30s (perhaps with good reason, having worked with Barry Manilow and the Nolan Sisters) and headed for a rural retreat in Cornwall. Some overgrown gardens in a nearby country estate caught his eye and led to the uncovering of the Lost Gardens of Heligan, which he restored and developed into a major tourist attraction with 350,000 visitors a year.

The Lost Gardens captured the public's imagination and fired Smit's passion for ecology and the environment. It also generated new employment and income for one of the poorest rural areas in the country.

The same factors figured in Smit's next undertaking, the Eden Project, only more so: 'We wanted to find the most derelict place on earth and create life in it.'[6] In the event, Smit opted for one of Cornwall's many disused china clay pits, which have left deep scars and a legacy of pollution in an otherwise beautiful landscape. His idea was to construct an enormous greenhouse to showcase the world's climatic zones and their plantlife, and to educate visitors about our relationship with plants and dependence on them.

His timing could not have been better, as the government was ploughing investment into major projects to celebrate the impending millennium. Smit knew this was the moment. In his book *Eden* he describes the complex balancing act he had to perform in order to build what became a £130 million project from scratch. His first public funding was a £25,000 grant from the local council, but by skill, persuasiveness and tenacity he pulled in favours from architects, bankers and contacts, £74 million of public funding, and an array of commercial loans to cover the balance.[7]

The project was constantly on a knife-edge as major funders demanded reassurances that couldn't be given. Its scale and uniqueness were such that the role of the social entrepreneur was to keep the faith that it could all be achieved and was worth striving for. Smit has an engaging way of describing this:

> *'I lead my life by two theories: Tinkerbell, which holds that if you can get enough people to believe in something it will almost certainly happen, and Last Man Standing, which says that if you have a degree of charm and people know you won't go away, they will eventually pay you to do so.'[8]*

The secret was vision and passion, and the ability to build trust. Smit also had the ability to make everyone feel that their contribution was vital, whatever its size or importance.

When the Eden Project opened in 2001, someone dubbed it the eighth wonder of the world. It became Britain's fourth most popular tourist attraction with 1.25 million visitors a year. And it has repaid its investment handsomely, bringing £150 million annually into Cornwall, creating direct employment of 400 core staff and 150 seasonal positions, and indirectly involving thousands of other people down its supply chain, which focuses on local suppliers as far as possible.

Smit is patently delighted to see his vision vindicated: 'Our social enterprise at Eden cost £130m and has already put £800m back into the Cornish economy – which is more than double the entire money that has come from Europe for the whole of the south-west. So to think of social enterprises as being piddling little things that you have to talk about in hushed library tones is nonsense.'[9] But above all Eden has become a hothouse of new ideas on climate change, ecology, housing and education. The overriding message is that social entrepreneurs need to think big: 'I would like to think that companies like Unilever, Shell and BP could be social enterprises. I would like to think that anybody running a social enterprise should aspire to being good enough to run organisations like that.'[10]

The man who made a new Eden has become something of a legend with his iconoclastic conference delivery – so much so that he is some social entrepreneurs' fantasy government minister. And he ended up getting the biggest greenhouse in the world.[11]

Little things that mean a lot

Australian marketing professional Eugenie Harvey found herself disillusioned. Despite an outwardly successful career in London, she realised that she, like many other people she knew, had talent, time and money but little sense of purpose. She felt she wanted to make a difference. After hearing a talk by community activist David Robinson at her PR firm, she decided this was the moment for drastic change and left to join forces with Robinson at his charity Community Links.

Here in 2004 she set up We Are What We Do, a movement that encourages us all to make small changes in our lives that add up to a better world. The book *Change the World for a Fiver* and the website www.wearewhatwedo.org offer simple everyday ideas to improve the environment, our health and our communities: shop locally, smile at people more, stop using plastic bags. Though modest, these actions give you pause to think and may prompt you to take bigger actions in future. For some people they may even represent the first steps to becoming a social entrepreneur.

So far so worthy. But surely it's only a drop in the ocean? Not at all. Thanks to Harvey's marketing skills and a great team, the book has sold over a million copies, and a similar number of people from across the world have not just pledged via the website to take action but reported completing their actions. The movement has gone worldwide and published a more recent book, *Change the World 9 to 5*, with ideas for actions you can take at work. And its next book is based on a campaign called smallaction-bigchange that asked young people to come up with actions they would like a million people to take.

Crucial to We Are What We Do is its friendly tone: a refusal to adopt the serious, worthy or preachy approaches so common in this kind of enterprise. Passion mixes with humour. And there's a well-thought-out strategy explaining how your small actions will combine with those of others to add up to something meaningful.

Harvey's success also demonstrates the importance of forming partnerships and securing support when you are getting started. She credits many different people and organisations for their contributions: up to 100 people gave their time and efforts free of charge to put together the first book, for example. And she has had assistance from top law firms and management consultants to help the organisation and its campaigns grow and develop.

Harvey's affluent, educated background and involvement in corporate PR have been a source of personal unease as well as professional advantage. But she's learnt that it's pointless to feel ashamed of not having suffered in her own life: it paralyses action, and people shouldn't let it stop them making a positive difference. Equally, not feeling good about yourself can be a great motivator too: 'I believe that taking action when you are feeling down is the best thing. In fact, my hot tip is to go and do something for somebody else.'[12] Not only will you feel better, but the people you've helped will feel better. It's a win–win.

Phase 2 of the movement will be about managing its direction and priorities into the future now that it is clear it has generated critical mass.

Eugenie Harvey: Q&A

What are your strongest entrepreneurial characteristics?
Determination, tenacity, a belief that it can be done, occasional naivety, creativity and eternal gratitude to the many, many people who have helped me along the way.

Why are you a social entrepreneur?
It's simply because I have a strong belief that we all have a responsibility to try and make the world a better place even in some small way. I like to think I am quite creative in how I go about doing that. I don't want to have to rely entirely on people giving me money, because then I am not in full control of my ability to do it.

What are the most important features of a social entrepreneur?
Belief, followed closely by passion, determination, grit and fearlessness. Oh, and always saying thank you to those who help you along the way.

Give me shelter

Pastor Pete Cunningham has made it his mission to find homes for South-port's homeless. Now in his 60s, the former stockbroker has almost single-handedly re-housed over 200 homeless people in the Merseyside seaside town during the past five years. But how did he do it? It's simple – he bought them new homes.

When he realised the scale of homelessness on his doorstep he took direct action at his own expense. He cashed in his savings and pension and bought a house. He then persuaded 25 other investors to do the same. They own the houses, homeless people live there, and their rent is paid for through state benefits until they get back into employment, for which they are given support. Furniture and food are provided by different charitable contributions.[13]

But Pete doesn't want to stop there. 'I'd like to see a £22 billion company that's housing all the homeless in the nation – it's a glorious possibility. If people could take hold of this as a vision and say, "These people need help" it could be accomplished – my dream is let's end poverty in our own nation.'

Are you neutral?

After a varied career in TV, the airline industry and PR, Sue Welland had grown disillusioned; she was 'unhappy with the value systems of large corporates, and about applying my skills to projects which didn't have long-term or real social integrity.'[14] At the time, environmental charities were starting to tell people how bad the problem of climate change was, but no one seemed to be offering tangible solutions. So Welland, with her friend Dan Morrell, set up Future Forests (later to become the CarbonNeutral Company) in 1997.[15]

Her business offers companies and individuals a way of offsetting the carbon they produce in their everyday activities. It can calculate the amount of carbon you are producing, advise you on how to reduce your emissions and enable you to offset unavoidable carbon dioxide through forestry and green energy products. It can even help corporations to communicate their carbon-neutral status effectively. The CarbonNeutral Company also has climate-themed products for sale to take the message to the consumer.

Welland's business partner Dan Morrell came up with the original idea for the business when he walked through a congested and polluted part of London and noticed how green the trees were. Hazy recollections of school biology lessons brought to mind the role of trees in absorbing CO_2 from the atmosphere. Neither of the partners had any particular knowledge of or expertise in climate science.

With her background in business, Welland was aware that 'You don't have a true idea until it's crystallised into a proposition that can be sold.' So the new company had to be creative about defining, packaging and marketing an intangible product so that people would buy it. This meant concentrating initially on planting trees to offset carbon and ensuring that the process could be verified and traced to an actual place. The next step was carbon-neutral flights and homes, and a project aimed at making Newcastle-upon-Tyne a carbon-neutral city. One of Welland's proudest achievements was persuading a major car manufacturer, Mazda, not just to market a family car that combines fuel efficiency with a package of offsetting to turn driving into a carbon-neutral activity, but also to make its own UK HQ carbon-neutral.

This particular social entrepreneur does her work through a for-profit company, arguing that a charity is not the right vehicle for a problem that manufacturers and consumers have caused. She brought in a chief executive officer fairly early so that she could become creative director, arguing that neither she nor her partner were the right people to run the company and that it was crucial that it would function without her management. This required setting aside her ego:

> 'I think the worst mistake in the world can be ... when the people who have the idea end up running the business. Don't worry about letting go because a good idea, if you're still influencing it, will translate into a good business if you have the right people there.'[16]

Sue Welland: Q&A

What are your strongest entrepreneurial characteristics?
Willingness to take a few risks, dislike of getting too comfortable in a job, love of blank sheets of paper and big projects, commercial acumen, no massive ego with desire to run the whole show, and a strong value system.

Why are you a social entrepreneur?
Love of life and appreciation for how short it is. Being more interested in the project and the enterprise than in being a billionaire.

What are the most important features of a social entrepreneur?
Engagement with people and interest in the fabric of society. The ability to inspire yet keep your feet on the ground. Knowing that you are different, but not making a meal of it, just getting on and doing what feels right. Commercial sense. Interest in networking. Drive, energy and being a leader, not a consultant. Probably having a partner – things are easier to do when you're in pairs.

A greener office

Major companies seem to be constantly upgrading their furniture and moving offices. In the process they often throw out perfectly serviceable items – it's usually easier to do that than find worthwhile uses for them.

Colin Crooks' solution was to provide a simple, streamlined package for companies. He set up an enterprise that offers a clearance service at a modest fee and passes on the furniture it collects to new users at very low cost. Green-Works takes unwanted office furniture that would otherwise go to landfill, repairs it and distributes it to charities, schools and start-up organisations. In so doing the organisation also provides work for unemployed and disabled people. Any items that can't be sold on or repaired are broken down for recycling or used for fuel. The companies donating the furniture derive benefit from being recognised for their corporate social responsibility.[17]

Crooks had a background in recycling, and had been involved in a project training unemployed people to repair old washing machines and fridges. In his work as an environmental consultant he had heard clients complain about the amount of furniture they had to dispose of whenever they moved. Second-hand dealers wouldn't take it all off their hands; they wanted only the best items. Crooks realised that the best solution would be to have a social enterprise that would take all the furniture and put it to good use. So he started small and grew his operation as opportunities presented themselves.

The key to his business model was getting the furniture free *and* getting companies to pay him for the privilege of having it taken away. But life wasn't always quite so simple. One crisis arose when the warehouse was full of furniture that he couldn't get rid of. No organisation he knew of seemed to want it. So Crooks used his personal contacts to spread the message, and luckily for him word of mouth proved more successful than formal marketing. Charities came flocking:

> 'That was the magic turning point for us. It proved that customers would pay us for a service; the charities were lining up to come and get the furniture. So the model was working, it was brilliant. That was the point where things really took off.'[18]

Green-Works now has four warehouses employing 80 people, half of whom work for franchisees. The model is capable of widespread replication. And it is delivering three bottom lines of financial, social and environmental benefit.

Colin Crooks: Q&A

What are your strongest entrepreneurial characteristics?
Passion above all else, but closely followed by drive and independence.

Why are you a social entrepreneur?
I've always wanted to make a difference. We face major social and environmental problems that are largely caused by the way we live and do business and I feel that the biggest contribution I can make is to show that we can counter these problems effectively if only we do business differently.

What are the most important features of a social entrepreneur?
Concern, creativity and communication skills. Concern about an issue, creativity to think outside the box to create a solution, and communication skills to involve the many people you'll need as allies, funders, customers and employees on the journey.

■ ■ ■

Let's pull together what we have learned from the characters and strategies of the social entrepreneurs we have met in this chapter and see what they might mean for you.

Am I qualified? You don't need to be an expert when you start out. Perhaps some of our social entrepreneurs are unduly modest, but these case studies indicate that passion about an issue matters more than expertise. Like Reed Paget, you can learn what you don't know as you go along. Indeed, knowing a lot about something can sometimes be a disadvantage: it makes you see all the obstacles in your way and stops you getting things done. Being honest about what you don't know will allow you to ask others for help.

So don't be afraid to get started, and don't worry if you have to start small. Jack Sim tried his ideas out at home in Singapore before taking them global. You can always scale up later; projects often grow in fits and starts, or by crossing into different arenas.

Am I a leader? A social entrepreneur doesn't have to run the whole show, as Sue Welland admitted when she hired a CEO. The key is to build a great team, know your own limitations and hire the people you need to make good your weaknesses.

How do I decide on a business model? Each of the social entrepreneurs we featured had to find the business model that would make their vision a reality. For belu it was a business that gives away all its profits – an appealing concept for consumers to relate to. Eugenie Harvey uses the income from publishing books to fund campaigns to raise people's awareness about the power of small changes.

What do I need before I start? Tim Smit reckons that social entrepreneurship is an attitude and a set of values, not a business discipline or a handbook to follow. Passion can find its expression in all walks of life and in all sorts of different ways before emerging in the form of social entrepreneurship.

Is there a secret I should know? Never give up. Successful social entrepreneurs believe that any obstacle can be overcome through creative thinking and tenacity. Colin Crooks extracted favours from everyone he knew at certain points to keep his show on the road. There is always someone somewhere who will help you out of a corner when you need it.

7

Seven types of social entrepreneur

'The social entrepreneur wouldn't be happy just to give someone a fish or teach them to fish – they'd want to reinvent the fishing industry.'

Bill Drayton,
Ashoka chairman

I t should be clear by now that social entrepreneurs can be male or female, young or old, black or white, rich or poor, famous or unknown, traditional or radical, locals or outsiders, ambitious or modest, high-tech or low-tech. But are there any patterns amid such diversity? This chapter aims to present a simple and helpful classification of social entrepreneurs in order to shape our thinking about how to foster social entrepreneurship in all its forms.

1. The social business entrepreneur

Liam Black and Jeremy Nicholls believe 'there's no business like social business' while Muhammad Yunus declares that 'social business entrepreneurs are the solution.' What are they so excited about?

It's this: once you turn a profit you are in control. You don't have to depend on the generosity of others. You can choose what you do and expand or contract. Grameen Bank could never have grown if it had been a charity; it had to be a profit-making social business.

How many charitable projects have you seen start up with a big grant only to close when the funding runs out? Or suffer agonies of uncertainty as the desperate search for funds consumes every waking hour and distracts everyone from their mission?

Roughly half the social entrepreneurs we have looked at are running a genuine social business (or 'hybrid for-profit') because they are producing both financial and social outputs or using financial means to generate social good. All the others may be acting like businesses, but they are not yet self-sufficient.

Muhammad Yunus describes how the social entrepreneur in this position has 'entered the business world with limitless possibilities... has overcome the gravitational force of financial dependence and now is ready for space flight! This is the critical moment of significant institutional transformation.'[1] But choosing the business way is no easy road. Running two bottom lines (financial and social) or even three (financial, social and environmental) is tough.

The Fair Trade movement began when a few pioneers in the 1970s and 80s saw that certain products could be traded in a new way to generate social benefits. But the object of the exercise – paying the producer a fair price – would entail higher prices for consumers. Would they be prepared to pay? The risks were considerable, and so was the responsibility to get it right.

Many of the moving forces behind the scenes were social entrepreneurs. One such was Richard Adams, founder of the Traidcraft charity and one of the key players in the establishment of Cafédirect. Backed by a public listing and share issues, this is now Britain's biggest Fair Trade company and sixth largest coffee brand with a market share approaching 8%. It has blazed a trail that others are now following as its giant competitors begin to adopt Fair Trade practices and branding.

It took social entrepreneurs to see a gap in the market and understand how it could be filled in a way that would influence the behaviour of other players. They found the leverage point – consumer power – and offered us products that do more for our money. The scale of today's Fair Trade market shows how far the idea has spread: at the end of 2006 there were 569 producer organisations in 58 developing countries operating under Fair Trade certification, improving conditions for millions of individual producers and their families and communities. The total value of the sector amounts to more than 1.6 billion euros, but there is still plenty of room for growth: in a typical product category, Fair Trade goods account for between 0.5% and 5% of sales. Perhaps more importantly, the concept has become firmly established in our commercial culture, with towns and even countries vying for Fair Trade status. Richard Adams was nominated as social entrepreneur of the year in 2005, swiftly followed by Cafédirect CEO Penny Newman in 2006.

At the opposite end of the scale, social entrepreneurs are tackling other market niches, but in a manner that challenges the whole way that societies operate.

Eric Samuels emigrated from the West Indies to the UK in the 1960s, settling in the Home Counties and building his career in the banking industry. But it wasn't until some thirty years later, when he came to one of the poorest and most ethnically diverse parts of east London to research a theology dissertation, that he was confronted with a need he couldn't ignore. There was no shop on a housing estate with thousands of residents. Getting to the nearest store took time and money, and even when people made the trip they were confronted with high prices and poor-quality goods. Samuels' financial experience told him that if no private operator could make a shop work then he certainly couldn't, and he ascertained that a mobile shop had little chance of being able to cover its costs either.

But he did eventually find a market-based solution: not some miracle business model, but a pragmatic ad hoc solution. He simply took himself off to one of London's biggest wholesale fruit and vegetable markets, spent a hefty chunk of his own money on produce, and sold it from a disused flat that he persuaded a social housing landlord to lend him. For three years the project kept going only because Eric was a volunteer. The produce sold well, so he always got his money back, but to keep prices down he never took a proper wage.

Thanks to a flurry of awards and public recognition in 2001, the project has now grown to a size where it can operate at a profit and support a range of food and health projects, generating jobs and training opportunities for disadvantaged residents at the same time. Samuels undertakes consultancy work and is replicating the model around the country.

His financial skills undoubtedly helped him to find the right way of attacking the problem and reject options that would never have worked, but he himself believes it was his motivation that made all the difference, and certainly stopped him giving up. His efforts highlight the shocking phenomenon of 'food deserts' – places where it is impossible to buy fresh (or sometimes any) food within a reasonable travelling time – in deprived parts of otherwise affluent countries. He followed his instincts, put his own money and time on the line, and worked patiently until the business became sustainable.

The lesson of social business entrepreneurs is that they have found a way to rectify failures in consumer markets by trading in them – a principle that can work in wealthy and deprived communities alike. Of course, not everyone can turn a socially motivated service into a business; if they could, chances are that the private sector would be doing it already. But perhaps income generation could be grown by 10%, say, or a separate trading arm established whose role is to provide sustainable revenue. Muhammad Yunus points out that many private-sector companies have the finance and skills to establish their own social business operations. These should preferably break even, but can legitimately be used to explore new and potentially profit-making markets.[2]

Doing good by making money; making money by doing good – now there's a new way to run a business. In this new enterprise space, innovators are finding fresh ways for financial and social returns to reinforce each other. The two are no longer mutually exclusive, but symbiotic.

Profile of the social business entrepreneur

What they do:

- Build a new business to overcome a market failure
- Identify a different way of creating value
- Aim for sustainability by generating their own income (perhaps after a subsidised start-up period).

Definition of a social business: 'A self-sustaining company that sells goods or services and repays its owners for the money they invest, but whose primary purpose is to serve society and improve the lot of the poor.'[3]
How they may start out: charity shop, local community enterprise.
How they may end up: independent business or partnership with private sector, market listing, commercial sustainability.

---

2. The citizen social entrepreneur

But not all social entrepreneurs set up social businesses. Some create institutions for social change.

Michael Young, who died in 2002, is regarded as one of Britain's greatest social entrepreneurs, but he focused on failures and gaps in institutions rather than markets. In setting up the Open University, National Extension College and School for Social Entrepreneurs, he was addressing gaps in educational provision. But he also knew that institutions had to be sustainable: they had to pay their way by charging customers, whether that meant individual students or the government.

Jeroo Bilimoria set up Childline in India to provide a means for the country's huge population of street children to get help in a crisis. To provide the service in the first city, Mumbai, she had to coordinate children's agencies, the state telecoms company and the police. The service has been so successful – open only since 1996, it takes over 3 million calls a year in some of India's largest cities – that the government is now rolling it out nationwide. It has become sustainable by becoming mainstream, rather than by becoming a business. But as a true social entrepreneur, Jeroo is launching new initiatives all the time: Child Helpline International has taken the idea to 71 countries so far and Child Savings International, a global network of organisations, will enable children to plan and save for the future. The pilot serves more than 70,000 children in India, using school-based clubs that prepare children to succeed academically, encourage them to manage their income and help break the cycle of poverty.

J. B. Schramm built College Summit in the US on the belief that education was the cheapest and best way to reduce poverty by getting disadvantaged young people ready for college and creating an academic culture in their schools. Those who made it to college would see their earnings increase over their lifetimes and their own children would be twice as likely to go to college. This persuasive argument gave public education funders a clear rationale to invest more heavily so as to reap the benefits later on.

Bob Geldof is a charity social entrepreneur. If there is one person on the planet who has made campaigning and fundraising for international development into a global art form, it is Bob Geldof. How has a former pop musician turned a complex issue like developing-world debt into an issue that most people are now aware of and sympathetic to? By being entrepreneurial: looking for a leverage point with politicians and the public. As he admits, 'I still had to have a business head on' – especially when seeking to ensure that the money achieves what was intended on the ground. Many campaigns have raised hefty sums of money but not followed through on delivery: Geldof the social entrepreneur would not tolerate that. He is a successful businessman in his own right with media, travel and marketing interests and has clearly combined that experience with his campaigning to maximise the funds generated for social change.

As a doctor in one of Rio's largest government hospitals, Vera Cordeiro became more and more frustrated by a recurring pattern of events: a child from a poor background would receive often expensive treatment for a serious illness but was then discharged to go back to live in a slum where their family lacked the resources to help them recover. This was both a human tragedy and a waste of medical effort. So Cordeiro set up Renascer to help these families prepare for their child's recovery, which involved working on the quality of their housing and diet and on family issues such as drugs. Such a multifaceted volunteer effort cuts across many professions. In the language of the entrepreneur, a child's illness could be the trigger point for helping an entire family.

Among social entrepreneurs themselves, there is a debate as to where the greatest potential for change lies. David Bornstein believes that the biggest impact can be achieved by citizen social entrepreneurs, arguing that by creating new organisations that are not necessarily businesses, they are liberated from institutional constraints and business priorities. Muhammad

Yunus takes the opposite view: business itself creates freedom from institutional constraints. Can they both be right?

Consider the hybrid social entrepreneur as social activist.[4] Kailash Satyarthi's RugMark campaign provides a striking example. Having made little progress in rescuing children enslaved in India's rug-weaving trade, Satyarthi attacked the problem laterally. He created the RugMark certification programme for goods manufactured under fair conditions and launched a public relations campaign to educate consumers about the problems in the industry and encourage them to buy only ethically produced rugs. Instead of building an alternative business, he is trying to harness consumer power to change the way that business is done in this sector with a view to transforming the conditions of production on a permanent basis.

There is a long tradition of entrepreneurial people working at the community level,[5] and the citizen sector can embrace everything from community projects to giant campaigns. This is a fertile area for social entrepreneurs who prefer not to engage in business directly.

Profile of the citizen social entrepreneur

What they do:

- Spot a market failure that can best be addressed by creating a new institution or adapting an existing one
- Aim for sustainability by generating long-term cultural, governmental or economic support for the new institution.

How they may start out: when creating a new organisation, trying to build in entrepreneurial behaviour from the outset.
How they may end up: managing a thriving new institution.

---

3. The public-sector social entrepreneur

Entrepreneurs in the public sector? Surely some mistake? Certainly we don't tend to associate civil servants with risk taking; nor should we, since they are accountable for spending our taxes. But in the search for more bangs for our buck, even governments are capable of innovation, often through the work of particular individuals who are able to achieve the unexpected by using business techniques to improve the delivery of public services.

Think back to Bill Drayton, dubbed 'bureaucratic entrepreneur' for his breakthrough innovations matching the needs of a government institution with the private-sector organisations it was trying to regulate. (And consider the political and tactical skills he exhibited later in campaigning to save the institution from savage cuts.)

Jamie Oliver's school meals campaign featured in chapter 1 puts him in this category. Fergus Chambers did a Jamie when charged with improving school meals in Glasgow's education authority. By emulating best practices in the private sector he created Fuel Zone: an attractive branded service across all schools that was cleverly structured not only to give children incentives to make healthy choices, but also to give the companies supplying those schools incentives to produce more healthy food. In the face of criticism from traditionalists and vested interests in both the education and private sectors, he and his team created a virtuous circle that served the health and welfare of young people.

Norma Redfearn is a socially entrepreneurial head teacher. A what? In the 1980s, the west end of Newcastle in north-east England had been devastated by the closure of the shipyards. Redfearn arrived as head at a failing school where attendance was poor, the buildings were frequently vandalised, many of the parents had themselves done badly at school and the surrounding area was run down.

She began by simply asking the parents what they wanted from the school. Then she tried to deliver it. One step at a time, she achieved spectacular results:

- The pupils had nowhere to play, so she orchestrated the community and an architect to create an award-winning playground.
- Poor nutrition meant that many children suffered ill health, so the school started a breakfast club and opened its own café.
- Local housing standards were poor, so Redfearn found a suitable derelict site and worked with the council and families to design it, giving priority to big kitchens and features that would discourage crime.
- Many parents were illiterate, so she found ways to involve them in 'second chance' learning.

Thanks to her efforts, this once failing school became so popular that it was over-subscribed, and acted as a hub for community regeneration. So great was her achievement that it helped shape government policy on the role of schools in the community. She had transformed not just a school and a community, but national policy.

The Demos think-tank calls people like Norma 'civic entrepreneurs': they are social entrepreneurs in the public sector. Identifying them and

Norma Redfearn: Q&A

What are your strongest entrepreneurial characteristics?
A can-do attitude along with positive thinking. Self-belief along with deter-mination and perseverance. Ability to listen and to work with others to achieve goals.

Why are you a social entrepreneur?
To narrow the gap between haves and have-nots. To make a difference and empower people to enable them to change their communities for the better.

What are the most important features of a social entrepreneur?
Having a vision that motivates and inspires others. Not taking no for an answer – there is a way forward, so find solutions. Taking risks.

working out how best to encourage them is one of the most effective ways of improving public-service delivery, Demos claims.[6]

A second major area where social entrepreneurs can affect the public sector and its operations is through partnerships. Governments are increas-ingly looking to work with both the private and third sectors to improve service delivery, and as social enterprises are close to their customers and can be responsive and innovative, they are in a good position to take on some of these contracts. Hackney Community Transport and Ealing Community Transport run several of the London bus routes on a not-for-private-profit basis and are able to plough the proceeds into additional services for the elderly.[7] Greenwich Leisure is a social enterprise that has turned around a number of failing sports and swimming facilities in that borough of London; local authorities now see similar partnerships as a viable solution to a common problem.

The main areas of partnership growth are in areas of high public spending where the dead hand of bureaucracy can often stifle results: health, educa-tion, care of the elderly, employment support. Social enterprises and a socially entrepreneurial approach by local authorities are starting to deliver a cultural change in locally responsive services, but they badly need to be scaled up. Done well, they can both improve quality and save costs: the Holy Grail of the public sector.

Commissioning services this way has had its teething troubles, but in the UK at least, it is now government policy to make social benefit a deciding factor in awarding contracts. This will create more opportunities for social businesses to grow and to influence the way services are delivered – and in turn help the public sector to be more socially entrepreneurial in its own right.

So befriend your local public servants and encourage them to find the leverage points in their sphere of influence: you will be helping them to achieve better results and to go places.

Profile of the public-sector social entrepreneur

What they do:

- Identify entrepreneurial approaches to using public funding to achieve its goals more successfully
- Learn from the best business practices: take risks, innovate and respond to needs
- Regard giving customers the best possible service as paramount
- Get to the root cause of problems
- Make large or small institutional reforms where necessary.

How they may start out: as a public servant looking for entrepreneurial solutions: partnership with a business or social enterprise, leverage of public funds. Or working with the public sector to encourage officials to take this entrepreneurial path.
How they may end up: initiating major reform of public institutions.

---

4. The corporate social intrapreneur

What does that mean? I'm talking about people who change the world from inside companies, *and* change their companies in the process. These are the private-sector counterparts of the public-sector social entrepreneur or, put another way, social versions of the increasingly well-recognised corporate intrapreneur – someone who drives change inside a corporate environment. They see an opportunity for achieving social impact by steering their employer in a particular direction.

Gib Bulloch did just that within the giant Accenture consulting firm. His employer had done no consulting work with development agencies because they could not afford commercial consulting rates and the firm itself lacked the relevant specialist experience and skills.

Bulloch was looking for a voluntary role overseas but could achieve it only under the firm's traditional frameworks of sabbaticals or charity work. On returning to the office, he realised that it would be better if his firm could actively support people in his position instead of reluctantly letting them go. So he managed to thrash out a new arrangement with his employer: the firm would elect not to make a profit on such projects, staff would take a pay cut in exchange for the opportunity, and the development agency would pay a greatly reduced fee to cover the overhead. A new win-win had been found: staff would be able to take advantage of an opportunity overseas that would bring them personal satisfaction and enhance their career, the firm would retain them and benefit from their new experience, and the agency would gain high-level professional consulting advice at an affordable price.

Bulloch used his consultant's perspective to spot an opportunity and work out how to increase the leverage. The strategy he adopted was to find a champion within the firm who bought into the idea, thus improving his chances of success.

He had to do a lot of manoeuvring within the firm to break so much new ground, but the system is now well established and all parties are reaping the rewards. Staff morale has been boosted, retention rates are up, and the work on the ground is proving successful. Though Bulloch gambled with his own career and had to take a pay cut, he reckons it was worth it: he feels the project 'takes corporate citizenship forward from just being about compliance, to an exciting and unlimited future.'[8]

This kind of initiative should not be confused with conventional corporate charitable activity (now often lumped under the heading of corporate social responsibility), in which business and charity are kept at arm's length. Companies vary widely in the amount of money they commit and in their own and their staff's depth of engagement. Gib Bulloch took Accenture to the highest level of engagement: a structural response where business and social mission blend into one. Though still rare, this could be the start of something big. Companies that see something good happening elsewhere are often quick to copy it – though the rush to be an early adopter can lead to oversimplification and tokenism.

One influential study claims that social intrapreneurs inside major corporations and financial institutions are critical agents for change because of the leverage at their disposal.[9]

Business guru Patrick Dixon argues that through example and partnership, not-for-profits can teach mainstream businesses a lot about the power of human motivation when properly harnessed. On the whole, people have a desire to do good, and the secret of motivation is a clear and meaningful mission.[10] Dixon has a simple test: *will this project motivate me and my colleagues in our work, and customers in their decisions and loyalty, by demonstrably making the world a better place?* It's a question that crops up time and again in discussions about social entrepreneurship, and it can be asked across the whole spectrum of commercial and social enterprise.

Profile of the corporate social intrapreneur

What they do:

- Steer corporate behaviour to make it more socially entrepreneurial
- May be able to create high levels of leverage if they operate within powerful businesses.

How they may start out: as employees trying to get social issues higher up their firm's agenda.
How they may end up: promoting next-generation corporate social responsibility by engaging and partnering social businesses and building social capital.

5. The environmental social entrepreneur

This is the only one of the seven types of social entrepreneur that inhabits a particular business sector because of the sheer magnitude of the issue.

The Stern Report, a major UK study of the evidence for climate change, describes climate change as 'the greatest and widest-ranging market failure ever seen. Its impacts are not evenly distributed – the poorest countries and people will suffer earliest and most.'[11] Mark Walton of Every Action Counts, a campaigning group that helps voluntary and community organisations reduce their environmental impact, argues that this is a key area for social enterprise to engage with, since it is essentially about addressing market failure and taking responsibility for the social and environmental costs normally neglected by traditional capitalist institutions. Two consequences follow from this reasoning: *all* social enterprises should be environmentally aware and responsible, and *some* social enterprises should have a particular focus on finding innovative solutions to environmental problems.

So it is no surprise that some of the world's most active and ambitious social entrepreneurs have chosen to work on environmental issues. We saw in chapter 4 how Nic Frances in Australia is facing the global challenge with an ambitious business vision. And as we saw in chapter 6, Tim Smit offers an educational and awareness-raising approach through Eden; Sue Welland a market-based strategy with carbon trading; and Colin Crooks a corporate-friendly recycling service. Similarly, Sir Richard Branson has announced he will spend £3 billion on environmentally friendly aviation technologies: this is not philanthropy but an investment, and one that recognises the market opportunity in finding ways to fly with a clear conscience. In combining business with environmental and social motivations, Branson shows a distinct flair for social entrepreneurship.

The environmental social entrepreneur is someone who looks for any and every possible way to change the behaviour of individuals and organisations in favour of environmental sustainability. To do so they develop a sophisticated understanding of the processes and motivations at work. There is a need for innovative thinking to get renewable energy, carbon trading and 100% recycling fully adopted at every level from local to global. Who knows: your local recycling idea may turn out to have international application.

Profile of the environmental social entrepreneur

What they do:

- Work in public, private or third sector, or all three
- Merit their own category because they may just save the planet.

How they may start out: greening their business or social enterprise by reducing, re-using and recycling.
How they end up: promoting widespread business and cultural adoption of environmentally sustainable behaviour.

---

6. The new philanthropist social entrepreneur

Business expert Charles Handy calls them 'a new breed of rich men and women turned social entrepreneurs.'[12] Mark Desvaux of ThankUBank coined the term 'philanthropreneurs.'[13] These 'social philanthropists' are spending their money not as the old-school philanthropists did, by endowing a library at their old college or funding an arts organisation that takes their fancy, but by supporting innovative approaches to meeting social needs to make the world in general a better place. And instead of writing a cheque and leaving it at that, they get involved with what the money is spent on, perhaps because they are frustrated with the way that charities do things. They view the money as an investment, not a support: they expect results, albeit social rather than financial, educational or cultural, and want the work to become as self-sustaining as possible.

This emerging trend is partly driven by what Larry Brilliant of Google calls 'sudden wealth syndrome': a new cohort of people who have become rich quickly at a young age through the public listing of their businesses –

The parable of the old new philanthropist

A long time ago a man started an estate agency in Oxfordshire. He decided all its profits would go to charity. He set up one that got involved in famine relief, another that worked with older people, and another that helped start up charities or expand them. You may have heard of his charities: Oxfam, Help the Aged and Action Aid. That man was Cecil Jackson Cole.

Do we just need more of these generous estate agents? Well, that would be nice. But the thing about Jackson Cole is that he was a social entrepreneur. He used his business skills to build long-term solutions to social needs.

In fact, Cecil Jackson Cole was a new philanthropist before the term was even coined. He was ahead of his time in addressing social issues in a creative yet businesslike way. Running a commercial business in order to create as much funding as possible for charitable ventures is one way of acting as a social entrepreneur.

people like Jeff Skoll and his former eBay partner Pierre Omidyar. Their challenge is what to do with it all. Less likely to be satisfied with conventional giving, they want to apply their business skills to the way their funds are spent, in the process reinventing the practice of philanthropy.

An organisation called New Philanthropy Capital was set up to help such people make better decisions about their charitable giving through an understanding of where their donations can achieve the greatest impact. Founded by City of London financiers Peter Wheeler and Gavyn Davies in 2002, its work is based on the belief that the principles of sound financial investment through research and analysis can be applied to helping funders support the most effective charities and helping charities to improve both the way they operate and the way they communicate their impact so as to increase the flow of funds.

Others may not be as young as the new rich, but they are equally energised by their mission. Successful Australian restaurateur Jeff Gambin had an epiphany when he talked to a homeless man on a park bench in Sydney, and ended up devoting his time and money to feeding and caring for the city's homeless people.[14] Mohammed Ibrahim, a Sudan-born telecoms multi-millionaire, is building a cancer-care facility in Khartoum in Sudan, but adding two floors of executive suites on top to cover its running costs.[15]

'Now I know why I make money' says Scottish entrepreneur Sir Tom Hunter, who is aiming to give away more than a billion pounds in his lifetime, mainly to educational development in Scotland and the developing world. And we saw earlier how Bill and Melinda Gates and Warren Buffett are giving even more — and not in a traditional detached philanthropic manner, but in a businesslike engagement with the strategy, directing how their funds should best be deployed.

Ram Gidoomal was one of the founders of Christmas Cracker, an innovative charitable enterprise run by teenage volunteers across the UK between 1989 and 1996 to raise awareness of global poverty and secure financial support for relief projects. As the head of a major international business he knew that the process was as important as the money. A Christmas Cracker chain of 400 temporary restaurants in churches and community halls up and down the country, and themed radio stations raised a huge sum and enabled 50,000 young Britons to gain 'an experience of social entrepreneurship at an early age so that it would become embedded in them, something they would never forget.'[16] Ram is now a professional social entrepreneur and new philanthropist, chairing my own social enterprise, Citylife, and getting involved in many other public and third-sector initiatives.

Profile of the new philanthropist social entrepreneur

What they do:

- Inject money and expertise into organisations and activities to maximise their social impact.

How they may start out: looking for an entrepreneurial way to give money at whatever level. How far can the money go, who will use it most effectively, can I get personally involved?
How they may end up: setting up enduring and innovative foundations and organisations, using their connections and clout to attract like-minded wealthy people to their causes, creating a lasting legacy and generally putting their personal fortunes to good use.

Don't forget that one of the people these new philanthropists might just invest in is *you*! So you'd better start dreaming, and preparing ...

7. The latent social entrepreneur

This means someone who has all the characteristics and potential of the true social entrepreneur, but doesn't know it yet.

Take an example. Britain's TV viewers were recently treated to the amazing sight of Colin and Justin, home makeover celebrities more used to snazzing up desirable residences, turning their attention to a tough Glasgow housing estate.[17] Would their techniques be exposed as shallow and superficial against the grim reality of a community that needed far more than a makeover? Would their reputation be tarnished by the presumption of even embarking on such a project?

In the event, the series made gripping viewing because of the journey Colin and Justin went on. After initial attempts to spruce up a few stairwells (soon vandalised) and organise litter-picking with a view to getting the community involved (but few joined in), they began to take more daring and thoughtful steps: confronting groups of young people on the consequences of their anti-social behaviour; getting key members of the community to take ownership and promote the ideas to their peers; and finding ways to develop impressive facilities for a café, advice centre, youth club and community hall. All this was achieved in partnership with the housing association responsible for the estate, so some money was available, along with a degree of official endorsement. But there were no blank cheques: further money had to be raised by dedication and effort. The whole enterprise was conducted against a backdrop of cynicism and disillusion among residents and housing association staff alike.

Somehow, though, Colin and Justin managed to win them over. The result was an uplifting combination of structural change and natty new colour schemes, to the acclaim of even the most jaded residents. Whether the change will last is another question, but the signs are good. Viewers were not left with the impression that the community felt it had been merely the passive target of a cosmetic exercise.

To my mind, Colin and Justin had put their particular skills and methods to a socially entrepreneurial purpose. Look at the elements: the task was too big to tackle by themselves, so they enlisted partners to achieve the desired impact, which was social as much as aesthetic. They paid close attention to financial viability: every stairwell had to be costed, every building enhancement budgeted and the funds raised. And they tried to ensure sustainability to make the project's effects last as long as possible.

Admittedly, this wasn't a case of pure social enterprise; they weren't setting up a social business with a paying customer base. But there could quite plausibly be a business in what Colin and Justin did, serving customers in the form of housing associations and local authorities that have similar problems in the estates under their care and an urgent need to get the most out of their limited budgets.

It's tempting to claim that professional social entrepreneurs Liam Black and Jeremy Nicholls would approve of Colin and Justin's efforts, since they argue that:

> *'the creativity required to regenerate a community on a run down British housing estate blighted by drugs, crime and alienation is every bit as challenging as getting micro finance to women in rural India.'*[18]

Maybe all our communities need a process for identifying and supporting the social entrepreneurs in their midst. Such people could be doing a host of different jobs; as Andrew Mawson says,

> *Social entrepreneurs are to be found in all sectors of our society — in business, in the voluntary sector, in the public sector: on the high street and in the boardroom and in ordinary living rooms up and down the country.*[19]

So where can we find them?

- In anything from a small company to a multinational corporation, seeking more purpose and meaning in their work and looking for new challenges
- At college or university, with the idealism and energy to make a difference
- At school, wondering what career or cause to dedicate their life to
- Working in a charity and desperate to think big and achieve more impact.

You yourself may be a future social entrepreneur!

Profile of the latent social entrepreneur

What they do:

- Realise that they too can become a social entrepreneur, and go out there and do it!

How they may start out: by knowing or reading about someone who is a social entrepreneur, by following their dreams and their instincts, or perhaps by reading this book and acting on some of its suggestions.
How they may end up: changing the world, fulfilling their potential, feeling satisfied with their career choices.

Qualities for success

We've already looked at the qualities of social entrepreneurs in earlier chapters, but the profiles of the seven types and personal stories help us to fill out the picture. For further detail we can consult Craig Dearden-Phillips's book *Your Chance to Change the World*, which draws on his survey of mainly UK-based social entrepreneurs.[20] Asked 'What are the key qualities in a successful social entrepreneur?' the 21 respondents came up with over a hundred words and phrases that can be gathered into the following themes, listed in order of frequency. (Again, don't let the list put you off – it's not a job description!)

1. Perseverance.
2. Vision and the ability to communicate it.
3. Passion and commitment to the cause.
4. Creativity.
5. Optimism and belief.
6. Integrity and values.
7. Pragmatism.
8. Flexibility.
9. Self-confidence.
10. Thoughtfulness (shrewdness, curiosity, intuitiveness).

Certain business-related qualities and abilities also figured strongly in the responses:

1. Business acumen.
2. Entrepreneurial approach.
3. Strategic thinking.
4. Leadership.
5. Team building.

When personal qualities are combined with business qualities, as we saw in chapter 3, the result is dynamite. One social entrepreneur described himself as a good all-rounder. But what such people really are – if it's not too much of a contradiction in terms – is multi-talented pragmatic visionaries.

All the 'facets' identified in chapter 2 are represented in some way. Some may be stronger than others: the social predominates, while the characteristics of focus, advantage-spotting, creativity and ego support the entrepreneurial behaviour and the ability to form, lead and inspire a team completes the profile.

Another source of reference is David Bornstein's survey of top Ashoka social entrepreneurs worldwide, which leads him to characterise the six key qualities of successful social entrepreneurs as willingness to self-correct, share credit, break free of established structures, cross disciplinary boundaries and work quietly, matched with a strong ethical impetus.[21]

If we put all of these characteristics together, we get someone who is:

- An ideas person (a creative and lateral thinker, an innovator, a generator of new ideas)
- A visionary (able to envisage the future and communicate it)
- Entrepreneurial (in terms of business skills and problem solving)
- Good with people (encouraging individuals, teams, relationships, networks)
- Ethically motivated
- Tenacious
- Confident but not arrogant
- Able to put all these qualities to good use.

But what about motivation? Is that something that you either have or you haven't? Clearly you can't force yourself to develop a life-consuming passion. You are more likely to uncover it, or choose to give it more expression. You can wait for a trigger, or you can consciously re-evaluate your priorities.

David Bornstein cites research showing that what separates highly successful entrepreneurs from average ones is not confidence, persistence or knowledge but the quality of their motivation. 'The most successful entrepreneurs were the ones most determined to achieve a long-term goal that was deeply meaningful to them.'[22] This meant they were:

- More systematic in the way they searched for opportunities, anticipated obstacles, monitored results and planned ahead
- More concerned with quality and efficiency
- More committed to the people they employed, did business with, or partnered
- Valued long-term considerations over short-term gain.

Eric Samuels sums this up well:

> 'What really gave me the edge was the drive to succeed. I really believed in what I was doing and that gave me the drive. If one door closes, I'll just go to the next one. There's always another door, it's just knowing where to go next.'[23]

What about ethics?

Social entrepreneurs are similar to business entrepreneurs in many respects, as we have seen. But their drive and strategy are harnessed to a different end. They have an ethical motivation that shapes and fuels their vision of a better world.

Bill Drayton believes there are two main factors that go to create a strong ethical motivation: a role model or someone who played a formative role in your life who had outstandingly strong values, or an experience of pain that compelled you to respond. Whichever it is, a pattern emerges: at some point in their lives, social entrepreneurs experience an event that makes them realise they have to do something, and that it is up to them to do it. And from then on they are fixed on it.

True enough, all the social entrepreneurs we've looked at have had their own personal moment of recognition. We can group these into three types:

- **Epiphany:** a revelation, sudden realisation or 'eureka' moment: 'the light came on in my head' says Jeff Skoll of the moment he conceived Participant Productions[24]
- **Road to Damascus:** conversion from one mode of operation to another (as experienced by several of the new philanthropists described by Charles Handy, such as Jeff Gambin switching from restaurants for the rich to food for the poor)
- **Excalibur moment:** a feeling of suddenly possessing the force or power to respond to a social need.[25]

These moments may be singular or cumulative, and precipitated by a crisis or an opportunity. Many social entrepreneurs who experience an epiphany speak of it in spiritual or quasi-religious terms. There are overtones of conversion, changing direction, making sacrifices. Many social entrepreneurs have a strong faith and regard their work as a vocation or calling through which they can express it: examples include Ram Gidoomal, Eugenie Harvey, J. B. Schramm (a divinity student), Nic Frances (an ordained minister).

Not just altruism

Concern for others is critical. But social entrepreneurs aren't saints. They seem to gain huge personal satisfaction from what they do – far more than they did in their previous careers, or than they could gain in any other way.

Bornstein describes social entrepreneurs as not selfless but 'self-*more* in the sense that they heed their instincts, follow their desires and aggressively pursue their ambitions ... On a daily basis they manage to align their interests, abilities and beliefs, while acting to produce changes that are deeply meaningful.'[26]

■ ■ ■

Social entrepreneurs set up social change businesses, organisations or initiatives.

They all use innovation to make a difference, and they are all businesslike in that they aim to achieve maximum leverage and impact, as well as sustainability. They tend to share certain personal characteristics, but these characteristics are expressed differently depending on the context in which they operate (public sector, private sector or charity), the vision that drives them and the way they choose to realise it.

Whichever of the seven types of social entrepreneur you think you might be or eventually become, you can take steps to develop certain characteristics that should help you succeed. We look at this in the next two chapters, which are about the practical 'how to' aspects of being a social entrepreneur.

Pause for reflection and action

■ Think about some of the people featured in the case studies. Do you see yourself in any of them? Consider your strengths and weaknesses. What do you want to work on? What motivation do you want to unleash? What influences from your past life do you want to respond to?

■ Consider where you are now in your life and your work. What can you do to act more like a social entrepreneur in that context? Which of the seven types do you feel closest to?

■ Do you need to move to a different environment to express your social vision more effectively? If that sounds like a big step, what barriers or opportunities do you face in your current situation? Is it better to stay where you are or strike out for something new?

■ What can you do to identify and encourage an active or potential social entrepreneur that you know? Perhaps they are working at the next desk, or about to leave school or college?

8

Do it yourself: 1. The beermat social entrepreneur

'Every single major strategic decision at Eden was made at night — by candlelight, and quite often by winelight. Decisions made in the day are made with a working person head on. You get working person decisions. A night person on the other hand will make radical and liberated decisions.'

Tim Smit, CEO,
The Eden Project

You may have read the bestselling business start-up book *The Beermat Entrepreneur*.[1] It has done so well because it takes a no-nonsense approach to starting a business. It doesn't pretend it's easy, but nor does it imply that it's only for the specially talented. The authors have distilled the key factors for success down to a few items that will fit on a beermat – just the job for when you and your friends get that brilliant business idea in the pub.

In this chapter, we'll borrow from this approach and adapt it for social entrepreneurs. We'll also look for great tips and lessons from successful social entrepreneurs around the world. What we are after is a set of transferable principles for taking socially entrepreneurial action in any context and from any starting point.

How to start

First, here's what you don't need: a business plan, a beermat or a pub. You may be happier sitting at the kitchen table with a coffee, or in the garden with a glass of wine. The back of an envelope is just as good as a beermat.

Choose an environment where you tend to get together with friends and where you feel relaxed and creative. What you *do* need, though, is passion for your issue and a hunch that you can do something constructive about it.

One organisation found that 50% of social entrepreneurs are personally involved in the issues they seek to address.[2] Do you use or help with any service or organisation that could benefit from the introduction of socially entrepreneurial approaches?

Look around you. What needs to change? It could be something close to home or far away. Who else is responding? What are the gaps? Is there an activity related to the issue that could be able to generate income? Or would the money have to be made somewhere else and then applied to the problem?

Think back to the social entrepreneurs we have met who rose to challenges. Now think about a challenge you have faced where you had to show initiative and determination to solve a problem. Maybe it was at work, in family life, at school, in sport, in the arts or in your local community. Perhaps you've been involved in a campaign or raised funds for some cause. Any or all of these experiences could be a great preparation for responding to an issue in a socially entrepreneurial way:

You identified a problem.
You devised a strategy to respond.
You had a vision of the solution.
You worked out what you needed to do to implement the strategy and achieve the vision.
You gathered resources or allies.
You worked, perhaps on your own, perhaps in a team.
You met resistance and challenges.
You kept going.
You succeeded …
… or perhaps you failed; either way, you probably learned some valuable lessons.

There is a pattern here, and it links back to the 'facets' framework from chapter 2. Each of the successful social entrepreneurs we have met:

- **Focused** on tackling a problem
- Spotted an **advantage** or opportunity
- Was **creative** in their approach to problem solving and generating resources
- Expressed their personality (**ego**) in the project
- Gathered a **team** around them
- Were strongly motivated by their **social** commitment.

The beermat method

As social entrepreneurs aren't so very different from the conventional variety, it would be a big mistake to ignore useful lessons from the world of business. After all, there is a long tradition of people doing business, thinking about business and writing about business, whereas social entrepreneurship is a relatively recent phenomenon that has yet to be documented extensively. So let's see what advice *The Beermat Entrepreneur* has to offer the would-be social entrepreneur.

Idea: Ask the magic question: 'Where's the pain?' How does my idea solve your problem? (There's no point having a solution in search of a problem.)

Person: If you want to do it yourself, you are the entrepreneur. (If you want someone else to do it, you are a catalyst, lobbyist or persuader.)

Elevator pitch: Capture your idea in a single sentence that can be easily understood by anyone. For Jamie Oliver's Fifteen restaurant, for instance, the elevator pitch might be 'giving young people from less privileged backgrounds the chance to be great chefs.' (When you acquire a mentor or key supporter you can add a second sentence to act as your endorsement.)

Mentor: An experienced person who has done the kind of thing you want to do. Once they provide the endorsement for your elevator pitch, you can take it to potential investors or supporters.

Team: Ideally this will cover five key roles. The entrepreneur (you) needs four supporting cornerstones: technical innovator (an expert on your chosen field or market), delivery specialist (operations), sales specialist (obvious), financier (cash management, cost control and relationships with funders). If you don't have the skills you need, grab someone who does: a friendly accountant, an administrator or a lawyer. Many people or organisations will give you or your team free help (see appendix for ideas).

First customer: For proof that the idea works.

White paper: Not a business plan, but a written account of what you plan to offer, its features and its benefits. Include if possible information on how people will use it.

Steps on the way

Any social entrepreneur setting up an initiative or enterprise is likely to go through a sequence of steps that apply whether you are starting up a separate project or business, or an activity within an existing business, charity or public-sector body.[3] The steps are:

1. Identify the problem.
2. Articulate the vision of a solution.

3. Devise a strategy to deliver the solution.
4. Brainstorm to test the idea.
5. Build the business case.
6. Assemble an initial team.
7. Network and build partnerships.
8. Gather resources.
9. Create an organisation.
10. Start delivering.

Or you might prefer to think in a different way:

1. It's wrong that …
2. It should be like this …
3. How can I get there?
4. What are the strengths and weaknesses of the idea?
5. How could it happen in the real world?
6. Who do I need to work with me?
7. Who do I need to persuade and get on my side?
8. Where will the money and people come from?
9. What does my project need to look like?
10. How quickly can I start making a difference?

The steps don't necessarily have to happen in this order. Things are usually more complicated in real life — they run in parallel or go round a few loops. Now let's take a closer look.

Improving school dinners step by step

The genius of Jamie Oliver's school meals campaign lay in its progressive roll-out from one dinner lady to one school to one borough to the whole country.

The campaign confronted difficult issues: the fact that poor diets appear to cause poor concentration and bad behaviour at school, and the inability of school meals providers (deregulated and working to very low budgets per child) to break out of providing anything other than the (generally unhealthy) food chosen by the young people themselves.

Oliver took one step at a time:

1. He persuaded one school to work with him.
2. There he had to win over the dinner ladies. But how?
3. He identified one of them, Nora, as influential among her colleagues and secured her support. A day at Oliver's upmarket Fifteen restaurant helped!

contd.

4. Having tried to create a healthy meal on the standard 37p budget, Oliver concluded it couldn't be done. This meant pushing for higher spending at a political level.
5. Oliver demonstrated again and again that his ideas worked by:
   - Showing the improvement in behaviour that could flow from one family eating more healthily for a week
   - Getting the commercial meals service to let him cook for the last day of term
   - Persuading the council to let head teachers attend a function at his restaurant where they could sign him up to provide their school meals every day (most did)
   - Training the dinner ladies at a boot camp so as to be able to start the roll-out in just six weeks
   - Taking on five new schools a week throughout the borough
   - Persuading the government to adopt this approach nationwide and raising the budget for each meal by 10p (30%).

The outcome was impressive: the government pledged £280 million for a trust to train catering staff, guaranteed a minimum cost per plate, and introduced agreed standards of nutrition.[4]

1. Identify the problem (It's wrong that …)

Ask the magic question for all social entrepreneurs: 'Where's the pain?' In other words, who is suffering, and what could be done to relieve it? And then ask 'Why?' to get at the causes.

What upsets, hurts or pains *you*? (The fancy way of putting this is: What's the market failure or inequitable equilibrium?) The entrepreneur sees a need and turns it into an opportunity. It may help if you have lived with this need yourself, or worked with those who have, but it's not essential. You may happen to know someone who works on a challenging issue and want to help them.

If you don't have something burning in your heart, do a little creative thinking to identify issues you are aware of, or cut to the brainstorming in stage 4 to generate ideas now. Draw up a list.

Five things I'd like to change:

1. ....

2. ....

3. ....

4. ....

5. ....

The one that stands out – perhaps because you know something about the subject, because it's local, or because you have thought of a possible way of responding – is:

....

Make sure that whatever you choose is something that you can stay passionate about so you will keep going.

2. Articulate the vision (It should be like this ...)

Perhaps you can immediately see a mental picture of what the world looks like when the problem has been solved. Or maybe you just have a strong sense that things should be different and an idea of what needs to change to make your alternative world come into being. This is your vision. It's an overused word, and inevitably a rather vague one since it describes something that doesn't yet exist. But *you've* seen it, and you believe that somehow it will come to pass. Your task is to take this thing you have seen and make it real for other people – otherwise it will stay in the realm of fantasy.

But surely visions like these are only for a special few? Not at all. Everyone has a notion of what would make a better world: it might be for ourselves, our family, our neighbourhood, people in need, even people on the other side of the world. Our vision may be buried deep under layers of disappointment, despair or cynicism, but we can all recover, discover or develop it.

So take the five (or however many) problems you thought of in step 1 and for each one try to add a corresponding vision.

	Problem:	Vision:
1.	....	....
2.	....	....
3.	....	....
4.	....	....
5.	....	....

My biggest, most urgent vision is :

....

Now you have your pitch!

If vision doesn't come easily to you, try one of these helpful ideas.

Write it down. Gib Bulloch wrote a strategy paper for his boss at Accenture which painted a picture of a future in which his project vision was a reality, with all the benefits that flowed from it. This brought the idea alive and made it more likely to be realised. When you do this, imagine it is for someone specific – visualise a real person reading it.

Time machine. Bill Drayton asked Vera Cordeiro what her plans were for 10 years' time. At first she was taken aback; she had never considered it. But when she began to articulate the possibilities, she found it invigorating: 'I'm beginning to see that if you think this way your dreams come true.'

Dig deeper. A good friend challenged Tim Smit to mark out a metre square patch of grass and then concentrate on it for an hour as if his life depended on it. He found it a profound experience, and it helped to deepen his environmental commitment. What's your equivalent to the patch of grass? Think about it and nothing else for a while. Record your reflections. What actions do you want to take as a result?

3. Devise a strategy (How can I get there?)

At this early stage, you probably don't have much more than a hunch – the outline of an idea for getting from the problem to the solution. So ask yourself a few questions:

■ What are all the possible ways to address the problem?
■ What is already being done about it?
■ What are the strengths and weaknesses of these existing responses?
■ What gaps do they leave that a new response could address?
■ What problems and obstacles would it need to overcome?

Creative thinking exercises may be useful here. The writer Edward de Bono has devised a number of lateral thinking techniques for unearthing unconventional solutions to problems; see the box on 'Creative thinking for social entrepreneurs' later in this chapter. Even if you come up with a solution that seems too outlandish to use, don't reject it yet. Bring it to the table in step 4.

Bill Drayton believes that 'Every entrepreneur, business or social, succeeds because he or she knows where the *jujitsu leverage point* is and presses towards it with every ounce of skill and energy. Finding this magical leverage point is the heart of the matter. The most common jujitsu point comes from demonstrating just how attractive a new idea is and then, through deft marketing, setting off a chain reaction of others rushing to capture these advantages.'[5]

More prosaically, try these 'marketing martial arts' principles:

- Leverage: use your weight effectively even if you are small
- Beat the sloths: which big and slow competitor do you need to beat? (Yes, even social enterprises have competitors!)
- Get the media on your side (use stories, human interest)
- Keep employees and customers positive
- Use viral marketing by getting respected sources to put the word about – it's cheap and it works
- Think of a good name
- Do the unexpected
- Plan for the unexpected.[6]

This may feel like advanced stuff, best tackled later. But the earlier in the process you can get a feel for any of it the better, as these things could easily influence how successful your idea may become.

Note that your *idea* doesn't have to be new (not many are), but your *strategy* may have a novel element to it. Or you may just be more determined to make something work better. Fair enough – that's how most progress is made.

I could get from the problem to the solution in these ways:

....

The way that seems most intuitively promising is:

....

The leverage point is:

....

4. Brainstorm (What are the strengths and weaknesses of the idea?)

Here's where you meet your public. You're facing your fiercest critics: friends and family. This is the pub chat stage. You need objective external feedback on your ideas. Sometimes people use brainstorming to generate new ideas, but your aim now is to use it to weigh and assess the ideas you've already come up with. Consider all the pros and cons. This will help you rank your ideas in order of importance or feasibility, or, if you just have one big idea, to refine it.

Your agenda should include:

- Is this a problem that needs solving?
- Can it realistically be addressed by the strategy I've envisaged?
- Is the vision right? Is it compelling?
- How can the strategy be improved?

Remember the rules of brainstorming:

- All ideas are equally valid.
- No criticism yet.
- Everyone must contribute and listen to everyone else.
- Look objectively at the pros and cons.
- Then at how any problems could be overcome.
- Finally rank ideas in order of value and practicality.

If you manage to get as far as strategy, well done!

Who should you invite to brainstorm with you? It needs to be people you trust. People who care enough about you to want to stop you going down a blind alley. They must be able to offer both negative and positive feedback. At this stage, avoid people who only ever see the downside: you'll probably need to win them round at some point, but you don't want them crushing your idea at birth.

If one or two of your brainstormers could turn out to be future team members, so much the better – you've hooked them early. You could also brainstorm with possible mentors, who are usually older and more experienced than you.

Finally, you can always use your brainstorming session to generate new ideas if the first ones don't survive or if you didn't come up with many in the first place. And don't despair if your original idea goes nowhere – a better one may be along in a minute.

Five people I could ask to brainstorm are:

1. ....
2. ....
3. ....
4. ....
5. ....

At this point you could also start informally pitching your idea to others, which has the double benefit of helping shape it (getting feedback) and gathering allies (getting support).

5. Build the business case (How could it happen in the real world?)

Whatever your idea, you have to understand it in business terms, no matter whether it is a school or community project, a public sector or charity scheme, or a big corporate programme. Why? Because in some shape or form, the problem you've identified will involve money (or the lack of it). Whether you are trying to improve school meals, make your school better, revitalise your community, transform corporate behaviour, reform government policy, or save the planet, you can't do it without money.

Lift the lid on any of the case studies from the book and you'll see the business case. But not many social entrepreneurs start with an MBA, so don't let your lack of qualifications or business experience put you off.

We have to move beyond the hunch stage, however, and answer this question: what is the market failure or gap, and how could it be addressed?

How well do you know your market (the need you have identified, and what is and isn't being done to meet it)? Who pays – or doesn't pay – what? Who gets – or doesn't get – what? What evidence have you got? People will press you to justify your assumptions, so find some relevant market research or do your own. You'll need to put together a report setting out the need you plan to address.

J. B. Schramm's business case for College Summit was that a college education adds roughly US$1 million to a person's earnings over their lifetime, and represents one of the best ways of tackling disadvantage for that individual, their family and their community. Accept this argument and you have a strong economic case for initial funding (from state authorities or businesses) to enable more disadvantaged people to access a college education.

Then ask yourself: how can this market be adjusted or redefined to achieve a better outcome and solve the problem? What money is spent on it? Where does it come from? What is done with it? Where does it go?

Nic Frances offers a good example of this process:

> 'I spent five years looking at [furniture recycling] as a social problem, and then five years looking at it as an economic opportunity. The economic opportunity is that every social or environmental issue has a cost. Understand financial cost and you can create a market, and then the problem will change or even go away.'[7]

Are there opportunities to bring more money in? (If the answer is yes, you are halfway there and have the potential for a real social enterprise!) Who might the 'paying customers' be: government, local authorities, health authorities, companies, users of a service, other individuals? Similar projects could have quite different users: for example, Emmaus sells recycled furniture to the general public to fund its worldwide communities for homeless people, while FRC sells exactly the same products to a mainly disadvantaged clientele who need to furnish new tenancies cheaply.

The key questions for a social enterprise, as opposed to a charity or purely commercial enterprise, are:

- Can it ever generate enough income to support itself?
- Is it sustainable or just a short-term project?
- Do we need to set up a new organisation?
- How do we balance the social and business aspects of what we do?

The business case for my idea is based on:

....

The market I want to work in is:

....

The main beneficiaries will be:

....

The main paying customers will be:

....

6. Assemble an initial team (Who do I need to work with me?)

Don't worry if you start small, with just you and a partner. It worked for eBay! Here's Sue Welland of the CarbonNeutral Company:

> *'Two heads are better than one. If you can find the right person to develop an idea with it's a beautiful experience with lots of brainstorming to reach the right idea. It also takes lots of blood, sweat and tears to make an idea come to fruition, and having a partner to share that with is a real help.'[8]*

Remember what chapter 3 taught you about the sort of person you are. In business, a simple form of successful partnership is between an ideas person and an implementer. Two ideas people or two implementers will not get far! If the implementer has business experience, great. But don't worry if neither of you do: if you're passionate about the cause, then you'll find a way to overcome challenges and learn what you need as you go.

Think about your friends, colleagues, neighbours and contacts. Who could you choose for your dream team? Who would make your idea a success?

Me, plus ....

and ....

and maybe ....

And who can I find to fill in the main gaps?

Expert in the field ....

Operations (admin, legal etc,) ....

Sales ....

Finance ....

If I had to start with only one close collaborator from all of these people, it would be:

....

7. Network and build partnerships (Who do I need to persuade and get on my side?)

For an idea to take off, you need gradually to widen the reach, improve the idea, gather the right backers. Your initial team or partner should be selected because of *who* they know as well as what they know. Who do you need to back the idea? What will make them more likely to lend their support?

The second part of a good pitch, according to Southon and West, is who backs your idea. Initially it might be only your mentor. What questions and approaches can you use to get people to help?

'I would really appreciate your input on this.' (Translates as: I need some funding, but your advice is also helpful.)

Put them first: 'You have the skills and experience that will really make a difference to this project.'

On money: 'Back this and you will be doing good and making money at the same time...' (if that's true).

The networks I need to be in are ....

I need to work in partnership with ....

8. Gather resources (Where will the money and people come from?)

The point of networking is to help you gather resources. Think about it under these headings:

1. Types of resource always needed in some form:
   - Money
   - Premises
   - Expertise
   - People (staff / board).

2. In the form of:
   - Gifts
   - Grants (with conditions?)
   - In kind (premises, vehicle, staff)
   - Loans.
3. Sources:
   - Your own pocket
   - Family
   - Friends
   - Grant-making charitable trusts
   - Government
   - Businesses
   - Churches or faith groups
   - Bank loans.

Here's where you're most likely to need your business plan or project proposal – it will help you justify your requests for resources and explain (to both supporters and the team) how they will be used.

Business plans vary in structure, but if you've followed the stages thus far you've got pretty much all you need):

- Pitch
- Problem (market analysis)
- Vision
- Outline strategy (new approach in market)
- Who backs it
- Resources needed (how much, in what form)
- Organisation and people – credentials, mission and values.

The experience of the Belu bottled water company is that when you are setting out to do good you can pull favours you'd never be able to get in commercial business. So ask for help with any of this. Is there a company we should be partnering with? Or a 'venture philanthropist' – someone who may invest in your idea by lending or giving money on much more favourable terms than any commercial funder, but perhaps hoping for a modest eventual return? Such a person may want to help you in practical ways too: mentoring, board membership, offering contacts and so on.

Just ask! (Or make sure your collaborator or someone in your team is great at asking. Ideally, though, you as the entrepreneur should do it, as you need to be able to sell and communicate your vision.)

The main resources I need for my idea are ....

For these I can approach ....

9. Create an organisation (What does my project need to look like?)

At some point you will need either an *organisation* or an *organised response*: a project, an initiative or a campaign.

In some situations you may need an organisation first, usually one that is registered as a charity so that you can receive tax-efficient donations. This can be a useful filtering exercise where you discover whether you have the persistence to get through the paperwork, or a huge source of frustration if you are in a hurry. It will depend on your outlook and the urgency of your situation. Some charitable funders will support you on the basis of pending charitable status.

But when speed is of the essence I recommend you incubate your idea within or alongside another organisation with the right status (probably an existing charity) so that you can get your idea moving straight away. You will also benefit from valuable advice and relationships. As soon as your project shows promise you can take steps to spin out independently.

What's the right structure? It's impossible to give specific advice, but you are looking for the solution that best balances your business operation with tax efficiency and credibility. The range of organisational forms in the UK includes:

- A company limited by guarantee (Ltd) with charitable status.
- An industrial and provident society for community benefit, which can raise capital through bonds and shares
- NEW: a community interest company (CIC), a company for public benefit that allows owners to share in profit while demonstrating public service.
- NEW: a charitable incorporated organisation (CIO), suitable for charities wishing to trade.

It isn't always possible to cover a full range of activities in one entity, so a hybrid approach is increasingly popular. Pairing a company with a charitable tax-exempt vehicle can allow each part to function effectively in terms of fundraising and risk management.

If you aren't sure what would be best for you, ask the advice of someone respected who is already doing something similar to what you have in mind.

Don't forget to think of a name that reflects your idea and mission. This will help make your project real.

The working name for my organisation is ....

10. Start delivering (How quickly can I start making a difference?)

At some point you will feel you are ready to start delivering your product, service, programme or campaign. You may already have piloted the idea and met your first customers. If not, you will ideally have lined up some customers even if you have not formally started delivering to them yet. Prior agreements and commitments can be essential in attracting funding. In my own experience at Citylife, we created the organisation in its legal form only once we had signed up the first 'customer city' for our social investment bonds.

Citylife

Citylife is a social enterprise that develops and issues financial products to enable citizens and companies to invest in communities and causes they care about. I work as its development director. Since 1999 we have been issuing community bonds in such places as Sheffield, Newcastle, East London and the Welsh coalfields, reinventing the old idea of mutuals and building societies for a modern era.

Spun off by Cambridge think-tank the Relationships Foundation, Citylife began by focusing on unemployment during the mid-1990s when levels were much higher than they are today. We have since widened out to a range of related issues: enterprise, debt, affordable housing, workspace – whatever communities feel are the key gaps in their local provision.

In the past few years we have moved into community property development and launched the concept of a social enterprise incubator. The Cambridge Community Innovation Centre offers a vibrant environment for developing ideas that help make people's lives better.

Our third strand of business development is to launch the community bond as a fundraising tool any charity can use. Some charities find that existing or prospective donors are able and willing to make a charitable loan, but lack any mechanism to do so. By packaging a simple solution in which all supporters are guaranteed to receive their money back, we hope to widen the fundraising tools available to charities and maybe even change the face of philanthropy.

Citylife's overall vision remains the same: to build a sustainable social enterprise and create a platform from which you can invest in making your own community better, wherever in Britain you live or work. The organisation's evolution continues to be unpredictable as it responds to needs, opportunities and challenges as they arise. The socially entrepreneurial bit is to try to make the most of the potential at every point – to punch above our weight. Time will tell ...

Issues in delivery include:

- Quality
- Timing
- Contract and clarification of expectations
- Learning from experience.

In the early stages, look for a customer that will give you time to gear up: a local authority or charity would be ideal.

My first customer should be ....

I aim to start delivering by ....

How long does this take?

All this will take time: typically from one to three years to get from your initial idea to an organisation capable of delivering on the ground. If you are in a real hurry you will be able to find shortcuts; incubation within an existing organisation or a supportive business centre is one. But in the normal course of events, the passage of time is a valuable part of the learning process. You may well be developing your idea while doing a full-time job.

The length of the start-up process depends on whether you are doing something relatively small as a sideline or starting up a big new business that might be worth millions. However, the disciplines of clarity of thinking and communication are essentially the same. That's why you must address each of the ten steps at some point, even if you vary the order.

Getting started

In the words of a major sportswear brand, just do it! (Which reminds me: think up a great slogan for your idea too.) It's easier to steer something that's moving. You can learn and develop as you go.

Do you have an idea burning within you already? Great! You can go straight to the development stage and start refining your idea. If you don't have a specific idea yet, just a strong desire to do something, you can search for ideas using the tools referred to in the box 'Creative thinking for social entrepreneurs.' Your starting point may be as small and simple as a single-issue campaign that raises awareness of a problem. A logical next step could be to address the causes or consequences of the issue through a socially entrepreneurial project. Campaigning can run side by side with the direct provision of solutions.

Creative thinking for social entrepreneurs

According to one view, creativity is innate and you either have it or you don't. But many people would disagree. The writer and thinker Edward de Bono has spent his life trying to demonstrate that we can all learn techniques that increase our creativity.[9] This is particularly valuable for social entrepreneurs, who need to keep on being creative as new challenges arise. Having just one good idea, however brilliant, isn't enough.

Idea generation, idea sifting and problem solving can be encouraged by disciplined exercises in lateral and creative thinking. Here are some examples from de Bono:

■ Adopt different-coloured hats to encourage different modes of thinking in groups: white for information, red for intuition, black for caution or negative, yellow for positive, green for creative effort, blue for control of the thinking process.

■ Get fresh angles on old problems by using the 'provocative operation' or 'po' technique. Put unlikely pairs of words together or pair a problem with a random word or image (e.g. unemployment po false teeth) and see what happens.

■ Make a list of unconnected statements to do with the issue in question. This sensitises the mind and allows new connections to be made.

■ 'Harvest' ideas by seeking to generate as many ideas as possible in different ways. 'For instance' ideas are deliberately unworkable but may spin off something that has value. Seedling ideas should have potential but need development. And comparisons ask what are the differences or improvements between the old way and the new idea.

Ask why

On several occasions, the Newcastle headteacher Norma Redfearn ran up against a brick wall with answers like 'You can't do that!' 'We don't do that.' 'That's never been done before.' Her response was always 'Why not?' and she didn't give up until she got a proper answer. Always asking 'why' is the route to creative thinking, and it's one of the reasons children are so creative: they don't accept convention ('This is how we always do things') as an explanation. Always ask why, and then you get innovation.[10]

Overcoming resistance

Technology innovator Anne Miller has written a helpful book about how to get creative ideas adopted and overcome the various waves of opposition that most new ideas encounter.[11] It is a human tendency to develop mental models of how we think things should be, and we need to understand that innovation often represents a threat to such well-established models. The key is to find non-threatening ways to demonstrate the benefits of your innovation. It helps to focus on the unmet needs your idea will address rather than the novelty of the idea itself, and to use a combination of facts (anecdotes and experience) and fiction (stories and hypotheses) to give the unconverted chances to empathise with the solution.

At what scale is it best to start? That depends on the nature of the issue, your own capacity and your strategy. You could start small because your time is limited, or because you need to start quickly, or because the issue itself is local and small-scale. Or you could start bigger or plan to grow quickly in order to generate enough of a response to make a difference, or to achieve economies of scale.

Onwards and upwards

Finally, I should probably add step 11, which is *constant improvement and development* – an iterative process that may double back to improve the strategy, solve the problem differently, identify and solve new problems and so on. You need to cultivate flexibility and adaptability, or as one of Craig Dearden-Phillips's respondents described it, 'The clarity to move ahead with a plan – the ability to change the plan at every move.'

But it's not really an endless circle so much as an upward spiral. Your organisation or project will be evolving and (we hope) growing. All organisations go through a lifecycle with similar patterns, and the role of the social entrepreneur changes as they develop:

- **Start-up:** the social entrepreneur has to drive the project with energy, determination, commitment and focus.
- **Expansion and innovation:** in order to grow the work and get through the challenges of growth and change, the social entrepreneur needs to show steadiness, wisdom, judgment, innovation and flexibility.
- **Consolidation and stagnation:** systems and procedures are in place, and there is a danger of becoming bureaucratic or stagnating; imagination and creativity are needed to move things on. If a crisis occurs (financial, legislative, lack of experience or competence) the social entrepreneur must be able to re-evaluate, respond and re-plan.
- **Renewal and regeneration (or failure):** if the changes are successful the organisation can continue. The social entrepreneur may need to learn about good management practice or find a more suitable role, perhaps as a consultant. They may even need to move on. If the project fails, the aim should be to try to wind things up as painlessly as possible.

Whether things are going well or badly, the social entrepreneur needs to work out when is the right time to move on. There are few things worse than a founder outliving their usefulness; all of us need to heed the signs and be prepared to make way for successors who can keep the mission going. A true social entrepreneur will regard the mission as more important than their ego or personal comfort.

If the enterprise has been successful, the operation will scale up as its impact spreads from a small and perhaps local client base to larger numbers across a bigger geographical area. The ultimate goal for social entrepreneurship is for the innovation to be widely accepted as a new pattern in society.

How you stay creative as an organisation will be critical to your continuing success – but that's another book.[12]

Triggers of social change

Social entrepreneurs need to understand how change occurs in society. Malcolm Gladwell's *The Tipping Point* explores the link between marketing and the process of adoption that leads to widespread change.[13] Social entrepreneurs who want to know how to intervene in the process would be well advised to understand some of Gladwell's key concepts:

- **Law of the few:** before an idea can tip into widespread use it needs a set of champions to spread information and foster trends through early adoption, recommendation and expertise.
- **The stickiness factor:** this is the quality of an idea that makes people pay close attention to it. Marketing and advertising often contribute, but stickiness can also be achieved by unexpected means. In one experiment, students targeted by a leaflet promoting innoculation against tetanus responded less to shock messages about the dangers of the illness than to a simple map showing where they could get the jab.
- **The power of context:** factors in the environment that mean an idea is ripe for adoption, such as the rise in fuel prices making home insulation, solar panels or biofuels more economically viable and popular.

The social entrepreneur thrives on change. Any change, welcome or unwelcome, creates new challenges and opportunities. Equally, a widespread sense of apathy or fatalistic resignation to the way things are can create an urge to make things better. That's why some promoters of social entrepreneurs refer to their people as change agents or change makers.

■ ■ ■

The ten-step approach has been designed to apply to most cases. However, there will be times when some of the steps are more important than others. The point is to use them as a prompt to start your change and development process.

If this really doesn't sound like you, bear in mind that some social entrepreneurs are ideas generators and catalysts who get something started and then hand it over to a new leader or manager. Once Jamie Oliver had proved his idea by opening the Fifteen restaurant, he brought in professional social entrepreneur Liam Black to help develop the Fifteen Foundation and take it international. Imagine the story behind *The Big Issue* (see chapter 4) from Gordon Roddick's point of view: it would be about spotting an idea overseas, identifying the right person to implement it in the UK, and supporting him through the process.

Pause for reflection and action

- Have that brainstorming session *tonight* (or tomorrow if it's late). Go to the pub with a few good friends and come up with three feasible ideas that respond to social needs you are aware of. Make sure the pub has plenty of beermats!
- Carry a notepad and pen wherever you go in case inspiration strikes. Or use your mobile if it has a voicepad.
- Look for a mentor who is experienced in business and/or charity.
- Talk about your idea. Don't be afraid to share things with people: social entrepreneurship is much more open than the business variety because the ideas are seldom patentable and don't need to be kept confidential, and the need to make a profit isn't the sole concern. If you are a true social entrepreneur and your idea has any merit, you will want it to happen whether or not it's you that will end up doing it. People's reaction to your idea will help shape it. And be prepared: not everyone will agree with you, but this is normal. Many social entrepreneurs describe being regarded with suspicion or incomprehension. After a while you may even begin to enjoy this!
- Start a business that generates money specifically to apply to certain needs, or do this with an existing company if you have one. Or buy a business to convert into a social enterprise. Advantages include: great corporate social responsibility, opportunities for staff secondments, opening up of new markets, covering own costs, even making a profit.
- Support a local social enterprise in your area by buying its products or giving it contracts. Whether you are operating as an individual consumer, a corporate buyer or a public-sector commissioner of services, the more you can buy from social enterprises, the faster each business (and the sector as a whole) can grow.
- Ask your local authority what it is doing to increase the sourcing of products and services from local social enterprises.
- When you have gained some experience of social entrepreneurship, you may like to mentor a novice social entrepreneur to help them through some of these stages.

9

Do it yourself: 2. The career social entrepreneur

'We must become the change we want to see.'
Mahatma Gandhi (1869–1948)

So you've seen all these case studies, you've considered your own potential, and you like the sound of changing the world (or at least part of it). You may even have found that one of the seven types of social entrepreneur sounds a bit like the sort of person you could become. But if you're anything like me or the people I speak to, you'll have a whole bunch of questions buzzing around your head. Where can I get careers advice whether I'm at school, college, unemployed, running a business or working for someone else? What's the first move? Can I get paid? What support is there?

Unfortunately you don't see 'social entrepreneur' listed as a career option on any forms or advice booklets. That's hardly surprising, as there's an amazing range of socially entrepreneurial people out there doing a wide variety of things. But there are some patterns. These people all started somewhere, had to decide on their direction, learned from their experiences and found a way to build their lives around the change they wanted to see. In short, life as a social entrepreneur is not so much a career choice as a journey.

We'll divide the journey into three stages. There is the journey to *becoming* a social entrepreneur, the experience of *being* one, and the challenge of *developing* as a social entrepreneur. As this book is aimed at encouraging people to start on the journey, we'll focus mostly on the 'becoming' stage.

Becoming a social entrepreneur

I have never met or heard of a single social entrepreneur who regretted doing what they did. In fact, according to Craig Dearden-Phillips's research, many social entrepreneurs wish that they had started sooner. Perhaps those who have had negative experiences are less vocal or less candid. But when you look at the stories of those who made a bold step or changed their whole career in order to pursue their dream, you instantly know why: deep down, they knew they *had* to take that step. 'Pursuing my dream' is not the end result, it's the main motivation. These people didn't want to spend the rest of their lives wondering 'What if?'.

Some social entrepreneurs make a sudden rapid change; for others, realisation may dawn gradually. Contrast the drama of Victoria Hale's taxi ride with the logic of Norma Redfearn's painstaking assault on each cause of educational failure one after another. Jamie Oliver's Fifteen project arose out of a conversation with a friend who worked with problem kids and observed that their behaviour improved when they were fixing a motorbike or cooking. Oliver resolved to use his cooking skills and connections to help disadvantaged young people: 'I would make top chefs out of unemployed young Londoners who had never cooked before. And I'd build a non-profit restaurant where my trainees could cook.'[1]

Your background

If you think about it, there may be aspects of your background that have been preparing you to act as a social entrepreneur.

Bill Drayton's preparation was a long apprenticeship in the arts needed to build a global development system for social entrepreneurs: law, economics, history, consultancy, the public sector. Each experience added a valuable dimension that he can now put to work at Ashoka.

Nic Frances observes that growing up in an entrepreneurial family as well as a host of later experiences helped prepare him for his future mission:

> I was called a 'social entrepreneur' on a BBC radio program. The minute I heard the phrase I liked it and thought it described me. It encapsulated my training in business, my experience as a hotel and marketing manager and stockbroker, my work as a founder of a welfare organisation, the journey through ordination to become an Anglican priest and the way I was trying to use all of these skills and all of my learning to draw in as many people as I possibly could to meet the problems of social injustice we met daily in the place I was living.[2]

But experiences don't have to be positive to be helpful. Liam Black had a violent alcoholic father who left when he was three, leaving his mother to do cleaning jobs to make ends meet. 'This made me a really assertive, demanding champion of vulnerable, disadvantaged youngsters,' he says. Before becoming a social entrepreneur, Black worked in the north of England for Crisis, a charity for the homeless, and for *The Big Issue*.[3]

Your stage in life

Am I too young? Or too old? Or too middle-aged? Don't worry: your age doesn't matter.

The young social entrepreneurs we have met demonstrate that youth can be an advantage: you know no limits and have the freedom to travel and work before ties and responsibilities come along. You may well be more idealistic too.

After university, Tom Savage worked in financial services for just a year before deciding that the career mapped out for him was too dull to contemplate. He struck out on his own and set up Bright Blue Ventures as a social company focusing on marine conservation. By the age of 26 he had started the TipThePlanet website[4] to change people's environmental behaviour and had established Bright Green Talent,[5] a specialist recruitment agency for young people interested in jobs in the environmental and corporate responsibility fields. Why not give them a call?

Older starters like John Bird (comfortably mid-life at 45 when he set up *The Big Issue*) often need all their experience and contacts to get something moving. Many of the new philanthropists are older still, in their 50s and 60s. Early retirement offers great potential to use your experience and perhaps give expression to an entrepreneurial streak that you had to suppress in your former career. And you may have acquired strong views about what needs to change in the world – and how – that will motivate you to make a big impact quickly.

But why retire? Life expectancy is increasing in much of the developed world, and an ageing population is likely to enjoy wider opportunities for productive later years. PrimeTimers helps experienced business people find new careers or service opportunities in the third sector, and advises 'sector swappers' on how to make a successful transition.[6] And at a time when pension entitlements are dwindling for many people, part-time work after the statutory retirement age can provide a useful additional income as well as representing a valuable form of social engagement.

If you need any more persuading, read *Careers Un-Ltd* by two great social entrepreneurs, Jonathan Robinson (who was only 22 when he wrote it) and Carmel McConnell (who had the older and wiser head).[7] They contrast the traditional 'Ltd' career mode with the excitement and potential of an 'Un-Ltd' future where you can give your desires and potential free rein.

Your choice

Those who are already social entrepreneurs have the luxury of being able to look back and pinpoint their particular turning point and what led up to it. Do you have to wait until yours comes along? No, you have the chance to plan ahead. You can think about what route you want to take.

Do I need to gain a particular type of experience before I begin? How long will it take? Should I look for a socially entrepreneurial situation or strike out on my own? Take a good look at yourself, your situation and your attitude to risk. If you're young you may have the freedom to do what you like, but perhaps not the money. If you're older you may have a different kind of freedom: savings in the bank, the mortgage paid off, the kids left home, and the chance of early retirement.

To me the choice is clear: whatever age you are, if you already have the desire to be a social entrepreneur you should go for it as soon as you can. If you're younger, you may need to think about securing additional experience and/or some financial security before you begin. If you're older and social entrepreneurship would be a second or later career for you, finances may be less of a problem.

Ask yourself:

- What would I be good at?
- What experiences have I already had that would be relevant?
- What further experience would be most useful?
- What's my motivation? Am I truly committed to this new opportunity, or am I just looking to escape from my current role?

Let's look at strategies you can adopt to reduce the risk of committing to a full-time role as a social entrepreneur. Here are some ways that you can begin to explore your new vocation without getting in too deep:

- **Start as a volunteer.** Help out at a charity where the work or the attitude is exciting and challenging, or become one of its trustees. Volunteers can help in all sorts of ways, from getting their hands dirty to fundraising to informal consultancy.
- **Opt for the portfolio solution.** Fit in social entrepreneurship part-time alongside other part-time or consulting roles (the Charles Handy approach): a mix of profit and non-profit activities.

- **Take a year out.** This could be a student gap year, a sabbatical or a career break from your employer with the option of returning to your old job.
- **Persuade your boss.** Find a way to get your current employer to believe in your idea and support it.
- **Pick the best stage of life.** Become a social entrepreneur before you have major responsibilities (on leaving school, college or university), or do it later in life when your responsibilities may be less pressing.

There are various starting points and intermediate steps you could take, but it may help to visualise the process in a diagram.

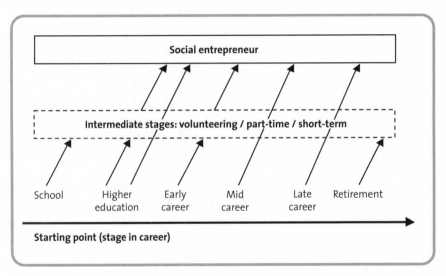

Steps from here to there

Still unsure? Take a look at Careershifters: inspiring stories of people changing to more satisfying ethical careers.[8]

Money, security, prospects?

These days most of us have got used to the idea that we are unlikely to have a job for life. People are more used to change, and many prefer it to the idea of spending their career in one organisation. This is a good starting point for the social entrepreneur's journey. There is also a 'post-materialist' shift in the values of younger people in particular: a search for different forms of meaning and reward than those that were available to a previous generation. Read *Careers Un-Ltd* if you want to understand what this looks and feels like. And as levels of formal political engagement decline, whether in party membership or voter turnout, those looking for other ways to make a difference need to know what avenues are open to them.

Even if money is not the motivation for the social entrepreneur, a certain amount of it is essential. In the better-run third-sector organisations, pay and conditions can be comparable with parts of the public sector or academia.

If you are striking out on your own and starting something from scratch, you'll need to work out how much income you need and how and where you can raise it. That's why I recommend starting in a portfolio way and making a switch to a full-time commitment only when you can see a clear path ahead: perhaps after a particular start-up grant or other funding has been secured. If you are doing something really good, there will nearly always be a way of finding funding for it. If you are entrepreneurial, the ability to locate that money will be one of your skills.

And as social entrepreneurship becomes better understood and more credible (and even, unexpectedly, more lucrative, as we'll see by the end of the book), it may be that your talent and commitment will be increasingly respected and rewarded in career terms.

Once you have started the journey you meet so many amazing people that opportunities are bound to come your way. Just get talking. And remember, the main thing is that you will be in control of your own destiny.

What happens if I fail? Try again! With any luck, you won't have lost a load of your own money or anyone else's – it's not like running a conventional business. In any case, social enterprises tend to have higher success and survival rates than small for-profit businesses.[9] And take heart from someone who has been there: 'Looking back I couldn't have done certain things more wrong.' That was Jamie Oliver talking about the first restaurant in the Fifteen chain. The point is to learn from mistakes and keep going – find another way.

There are four key groups of people I want to encourage to have the confidence to start the social entrepreneur journey: young people at school, students, charity workers and business people.

Young people at school

Here's Jamie again with encouragement for young people from his school experience:

Having not been the brightest banana in the bunch myself, I realised that my biggest weapon in life was the determination, enthusiasm, hands-on and 'actions speak louder than words' approach my father taught me, and I wanted to get this across to others, especially those interested in food.[10]

It's not about brain power or exam results, it's about passion. Like Jamie Oliver, you are young and idealistic. Maybe you've looked at social enterprise in your business studies curriculum, or run a mini-business with the Young Enterprise charity that visits your school. But what do you do next? Your careers adviser is unlikely to recommend that you go into social entrepreneurship.

I asked Jeff Skoll how he would advise young people to get started and he recommended trying to write your own obituary. It motivated him to achieve things that were important and meaningful in his life.

Michael Norton, founder of Youthbank, an awards fund run by young people to support local projects designed by young people to improve their communities,[11] says simply:

'Go with your passion. The key value is wanting to build a better world. The biggest problem is apathy: feeling that you can't do anything. Just get up and do it. You'll become a more interesting person. You'll learn from your experience and you'll succeed.'[12]

And it's OK to be a bit selfish: 'Changing the world is fun.'

Eugenie Harvey, the inspiration behind We Are What We Do, says this:

'Believe that change is possible. The world can and will be a better place - but we need you to help us achieve it. Please harness your idealism and energy and use them in whatever way you can to create a safer, happier, more just world.'

And Colin Crooks keeps it short and snappy: 'Ask where you can put your energies and talents to make the biggest difference.'

Some great things are beginning to happen in the UK to encourage young people to think along these lines. The government has launched a set of helpful initiatives over the past few years:

- The UnLtd Foundation to support and fund new socially enterprising ideas, with a special focus on young people
- Social Enterprise Day every November
- The Make Your Mark with a Tenner campaign, in which 10,000 young people are given £10 each and challenged to turn it into more through an enterprise with a social focus

- The inclusion of social enterprise in the school business studies curriculum
- A Commission for Youth Social Enterprise to report on how to over-come the barriers that prevent young people from becoming social entrepreneurs.

Strong networks to start up and support young social entrepreneurs are also emerging elsewhere: examples include Bill Drayton's Youth Venture in the US, the Youth Social Enterprise Initiative in South and Southeast Asia, and the recent transfer of the UnLtd model to India.

Social entrepreneurs are starting younger, and even at school. This bodes well for the future. So as Jack Sim of the World Toilet Organisation says, 'Don't waste your time on futile computer games. The world awaits your leadership. There are *real* problems out there for you to handle. Identify them and solve them.' And as one of Tim Smit's collaborators on the Eden Project, Philip McMillan Browse, says, 'You can only achieve the impossible by asking the young, because they don't know it can't be done.'

How to prepare

There are lots of things that you as a young person can do to prepare to be a social entrepreneur at some point in the future. Here is a list to start you thinking:

- Help with fundraising campaigns
- Volunteer with a charity
- Join a campaign
- Read widely
- Look at social entrepreneur blogs such as Social Edge and i-genius (see resources list)
- Visit a social enterprise in your area
- Interview a social entrepreneur for your school magazine
- Study business or economics
- Do a school enterprise project such as Young Enterprise or Junior Achievement. See if you can turn it into a social enterprise by making it as ethical or socially beneficial as possible.

If you want to study further, think about steering your degree or diploma to relevant areas: business and management studies, economics, develop-ment studies. Engineering is useful for practical skills and project manage-ment. It's best to study a subject that inspires you; the place where your skills and passions lie may be the place where you can best set up a social enterprise in the future.

When you're ready to go into work, think about what experience would be relevant to your future direction. Retail is one obvious choice: you'll quickly become immersed in the world of products and services, buying and selling, promotion and marketing. Other valuable work experience to look for now or later would include working for a charity, marketing, research, accounts, project management, consultancy, public-sector health and management. Civil service jobs can give you a valuable grounding in how government works and how it tackles the issues facing your country. Care and social work roles will bring you face to face with vulnerable people. Any of these positions will give you skills and experience that will be useful in setting up and managing a social enterprise.

And a word to parents: you can widen your child's thinking to include these options.

Students

Undergraduates make ideal social entrepreneurs of the future. They are often idealistic. They are bombarded with facts and analysis about the world and its problems. They meet people from a range of backgrounds. They may be keen to join campaigns and groups. They have few personal ties. And they have the time and appetite to travel, take risks and seek out satisfying experiences.

At the same time, these young people are the future leaders and shapers of our societies. Not surprisingly, big corporations want to hire the best among them. And they have the resources to do so, thanks to careers fairs, tempting starting packages and the promise of advancement. Your degree gives you something they want: the ability to think. And with student debt an issue in most countries, you probably need to get earning.

This poses a dilemma. Do you take the corporate dollar and abandon your principles, or follow your heart and do a meaningful but lower-paid job? This is one of the questions being grappled with by students at Cambridge University, who have set up a Social Entrepreneur Community to raise awareness of this growing field and challenge their peers to consider it for a career. They have toured the country interviewing social entrepreneurs and making a video of their life stories to inspire people.[13] Already coming up with ideas and projects, they may well turn into creative and socially minded influencers during their careers.

Some of the questions the students have asked me include: is social entrepreneurship a career? How do I get started? Can I make a living? What jobs are available? These are real issues for students, many of whom have a world of choices at their disposal and face family and peer pressure to be successful, yet want to avoid ending up in an unsatisfying conventional career. But the career path of the social entrepreneur is not straightforward, nor is the advice simple. Some people go straight into the third sector, perhaps setting up their own social enterprise. Others will be happier and more effective if they get the right business or public-sector experience first. Of course, it is possible to do things the other way round: a student who shows enough initiative to set up a social venture may stand out as an attractive new hire in the eyes of a future commercial employer.

Work out where you want to be in five or ten years' time, and then decide which stepping stones will get you there. The principle is to look for work experience for the time you need to learn key skills, generate some income and establish a base. And make a pact with yourself, or with a few good friends, that you won't get sucked into the corporate lifestyle for too long and forget your plan to use it as a springboard into social change.

Take inspiration from those who have travelled that path before, and recognise the potential you have within you. Colin Crooks challenges you to 'ask the hard questions about how your chosen field of study can impact for good: what lessons can be drawn from history, politics, engineering, science and so on that can inspire and create positive change?'

And Jack Sim reminds you to follow your instincts: 'The university has now made you think in a structured way. It can be very stifling at times to think like an academic. Try not to stay inside the box. Do what you think is naturally good and obviously good. Retain your common sense. Don't rely on fixed format too much.'

You are one of the next generation of leaders, the influencers of the future. Start being socially entrepreneurial and nurturing your potential *now*.

Actions you can take now

Here are some suggestions to get you moving:

- Reassess your choice of degree subject; switch courses or select helpful modules
- Join relevant student societies
- Travel widely to experience different cultures and social challenges
- Join or set up a social entrepreneur group in your university or college
- Consider graduate trainee positions: they can give you a lot of experience very quickly.

Business people

'Come on you business people who only manage one bottom line!'[14] There are two basic options for business people to consider: to be more socially entrepreneurial in their current business, or to make a complete change into social entrepreneurship.

Business experience gives you a great starting point for becoming a social entrepreneur. You will know about the key disciplines of running an organisation and getting products and services to market. To move towards social entrepreneurship you could:

- Support social entrepreneurs through your charity budget or by giving staff time: it will make the money go further and motivate the staff involved. You may be able to structure the funding so you get some or all of it back if it goes into an income-generating social enterprise.
- Adopt socially entrepreneurial approaches in your business model. A partnership with a charity or social enterprise could be good for business too – it may even open up a new market.

This is good corporate social responsibility with an entrepreneurial twist – it can be good business too. Surely this is how all entrepreneurs should do their CSR? Here's Jack Sim on responsibility:

'Life is not a scoreboard. You are capable of business excellence and also your care for society. Involve your staff in social work. People who work for a purpose work better than those who only work for money.'

And as Jeff Skoll puts it:

'For business people, doing well and doing good go hand in hand ... Businesses that support social causes gain happier employees and more loyal customers ... the more support there is, the better it goes.'

Getting the balance right can be dynamite. If you need any more persuading, Colin Crooks pitches in with the environmental challenge: 'Take time out and seriously question whether your product or service can remain viable in its current form in a world of more expensive energy and scarcer resources.' It's time for innovation. Richard Branson seems to have been through a similar thought process leading to his investment in environmental technologies and in setting up Virgin Unite, a charitable foundation that has social business as one of its themes.

Bill Gates is responding to the call even more dramatically. In 2008 he moved out of his day-to-day leadership role with Microsoft in order to devote more time to working with his foundation. As a seasoned entrepreneur he is not satisfied with simply handing his money over to someone else; he needs to be in control. And we have already seen that he wants to apply business principles to make his money achieve maximum impact. Could Bill Gates be the ultimate global businessman bent on making the transition to social entrepreneur?

Actions you can take now

Some ideas to start you off:

- Try socially entrepreneurial corporate social responsibility with your company's money and staff time. Look for the win-win.
- Get personally involved in social entrepreneurship. Maybe start with a foot in both camps: keep your business going and set up a social business within or alongside it. Or consider adopting a social business. Use your commercial business to generate cash for new social ventures.
- In the UK you could consider converting your company into a Community Interest Company. Dividends will be capped and you will need the approval of your shareholders, but you may find you get greater long-term satisfaction and customer appreciation from being in the vanguard of officially recognised social and ethical businesses.
- Learn about the culture and challenges of the third sector. Charity law makes this a place all of its own, and many organisations are bogged down with issues of funding and governance. Business people can inject new dynamism.

Charity workers

If social entrepreneurship calls on business people to become more socially oriented, it equally calls on socially motivated people to become more businesslike. The two fields must converge. What social entrepreneurship requires of people working in the charity sector is to look for ways to make their work more self-sufficient. This can have an impact on your career because you will be at the forefront of change.

Many social entrepreneurs, actual or potential, are already working in the third sector. It's fertile ground, as passion and commitment are key qualities for success. The question is, how far do you want to take it?

If your organisation is always struggling for funding, or if it is working in an area with room for growth, exploring social entrepreneurship may offer an answer. But this will be a cultural change, and not all your colleagues, trustees or supporters may be ready for it. You will be asking: how can we be more enterprising? What can we develop in our charity that will make it more successful and sustainable to help us deliver on our mission? At the same time, how do I as a person grow into this role and develop my career?

Eye care

The Aravind eye clinic in India was started on a small charitable scale by Dr G. Venkataswamy in 1976 and has grown into the largest eye-care centre in the world, treating over 1.7 million patients each year, two-thirds of them for free. Its model? A social enterprise where the fees of the richer patients also pay for the operations of the poorer.

One of the reasons that charity staff need to consider how socially entrepreneurial they and their organisations can become is that the rapid expansion of the sector may become unsustainable. The third or citizen sector is growing at an unprecedented rate, particularly in countries that have recently embraced democracy.

- The number of charities in the UK has almost doubled from 98,000 in 1991 to 170,000 in 2007: that's more than 4,000 new charities per year.
- Brazil's citizen organisations jumped from 250,000 to 400,000 during the 1990s alone, a growth rate of 60%.
- In the US, tax-registered public service groups grew at a similar pace, increasing from 464,000 to 734,000 during the same decade.
- Indonesia had one environmental NGO in 1985 but now has over 2,000.
- India has over a million citizen organisations and the US around 2 million.[15]

Wherever you look, the numbers are growing. Many will fail because they can't generate enough income to sustain themselves. Voluntary associations with a low cost base have less of a challenge, but as soon as you need paid staff to deliver high-quality services you are on a different level. Organisations that begin because someone has found an individual donor to get started always struggle if that donor isn't able or chooses not to continue their support. Philanthropic money is finite, and to win you need to be great at fundraising. Charities that survive often spend disproportionate amounts of management time chasing the next grant.

eBay founder Pierre Omidyar has commented that private capital is 'essentially limitless.' Few charities can secure finance from this source at the moment, but both charities and investors are changing. Venture philanthropy is becoming more common. Major charities like Oxfam have developed a more socially entrepreneurial culture across the board, as well as setting up specific social enterprise projects. Even traditional grant-makers are demanding more accountability, better outcome measurement and sound management practices among the organisations they fund.

The UK is moving to a loan or quasi-equity culture for the funding of major social enterprises or charities whereby bodies such as Futurebuilders and Adventure Capital Fund will advance larger sums to enable organisations to scale up and deliver bigger public-sector contracts or their own programmes, such that the capital can be repaid over time. A similar approach (except that the funding is not repayable) is taken by the innovative Impetus Trust, which injects both capital and expertise in a structured way to help social enterprises grow.

In principle, vast funds could become available for those third-sector organisations that can demonstrate they are ready for them, will make best use of them and can even grow them – in other words, those that are socially entrepreneurial. But there are some hard questions to face:

- Should my organisation ever take a loan, however generous the terms?
- Can *any* charity do social enterprise?
- Should my charity set up a new social enterprise?
- How do I guard against 'mission drift'?

These are legitimate concerns. Many charities are averse to loans because of the perceived risks they bring, and accepting them can be a big step for traditional trustees to make. But it may be the only way of growing, and could be the right choice as long as the business plan for the use of the money is sound. Some charities will always be more comfortable sticking to what they feel they are best at, especially where they have a steady income stream from reliable donor sources or an endowment of money or property. And setting up a new organisation isn't always a good idea. Impressive though it may seem, it can consume an enormous amount of effort and distract management, and it may not last.

But as examples and experience multiply, the opportunities for charities to behave more entrepreneurially will become better understood, and those who learn to overcome the difficulties may be the ones that achieve the greatest long-term impact.

Advice from old hands

Here are some insights from a few of the social entrepreneurs I consulted while writing this book:

'Non-profits have their overheads. Funding projects without overheads is not practical. Do both. Pick non-profits that are mission driven. People

contd.

who'll die for the mission. Don't support those who do it for self-interest. There are many non-profits who have drifted away from their original mission.'
Jack Sim

'Consider the value to your organisation if you had a trading arm. The business could directly provide a product or service related to your objectives. It could also raise funds to make you less dependent on handouts.'
Reed Paget

'Charities are notorious for not recycling and not tackling issues that are outside their core focus. Charity managers should take a broader view of the issues and reduce their impact on the planet in their operations wherever they can and even if the investments needed are not strictly in line with their objectives.'
Colin Crooks

Actions you can take now

Some suggestions to act as a starting point:

- If you are thinking of working in the third sector, target the entrepreneurial organisations. You could ask an intermediary organisation such as Ashoka, Skoll or UnLtd who they particularly recommend.
- If you are already in the sector, learn about social enterprise techniques: short courses and programmes are proliferating (see the appendix).
- Explore all possible ways of generating income for your work through trading. This doesn't necessarily mean that all your users will have to pay. Perhaps you could operate like Aravind: find a market for your services that can afford to pay more to yield cross-subsidy for your core mission.
- Consider whether increasing in size would give you cost savings. If so, how could you grow? Who might invest in your growth?

If after thinking about this you feel frustrated that your organisation may not be capable of developing any meaningful level of social entrepreneurship, that could be a sign that you should move on and set up your own social enterprise.

Being a social entrepreneur

Knowing that you are a social entrepreneur and being in a role where you can give full expression to your talents can be the most exhilarating experience. Let Fabio Rosa, leader of a rural electrification programme in Brazil, tell you what it's like:

> 'I am trying to build a little part of the world in which I would like to live. A project only makes sense to me when it proves useful to make people happier and the environment more respected, and when it represents a hope for a better future. This is the soul of my projects. There are easier things to do. But this has been the only way I feel happy.
>
> Creating projects, implementing them and succeeding, witnessing one's dreams come true, is happiness. To have a vision is to dream with a new world in mind.
>
> I am a slave to my dreams, thoughts and ideas.
>
> I need money to accomplish my projects. But money only matters if it helps to solve people's problems. My projects help people around me to acquire wealth and in some ways this comes back to me.'[16]

From these moving reflections and all the case studies we have looked at, we can see the source of true personal fulfilment in the taking of steps on the journey from the world as it is to the world as it should be. The journey is full of creative tension, but passion and purpose too. There is a sense of being in the right place, experiencing flow in your work, knowing the trials and joys of solving difficult problems, and building relationships with those you are partnering and helping.

To be sure, there are many frustrations, but your sense of engagement makes them all worthwhile. Being a social entrepreneur is a wonderful experience. At the moment, though, too few people get to share it.

A future as a social entrepreneur

The future is exciting. You are joining a rising curve. The social entrepreneurs I talked to are full of hope for what they can achieve and what lies ahead. Instead of resting on their laurels, they set themselves fresh challenges.

Jack Sim has set himself two goals: for every human on earth to have access to clean, safe and ecological sanitation, and to shatter the toilet taboo for all time. As for social entrepreneurs in general, he'd like them 'to dream big and get the support they need to scale up their good work.' He thinks social entrepreneurship should become 'a way of life for all businesses – not restricted to CSR alone.'

Sue Welland is equally ambitious for her role in climate change. She hopes to develop the CarbonNeutral Company into 'an international force which catalyses a step change in tackling CO_2 emissions' while 'sustaining a sense of maximum personal fulfilment; never working with or for something or someone I don't believe in or like; and to have made a difference.'

But you don't have to be a superhero and sacrifice your whole life. Eugenie Harvey says:

'My personal ambitions and dreams are (boringly) to live a long and happy life surrounded by people I love and care for and who feel the same way about me, as well as making a useful contribution to the world and those around me. My own dream for social entrepreneurs generally is that we all work together to help one another do better and better work and that in so doing, we make this a dynamic, effective and highly professional sector which attracts the brightest minds while remaining faithful to our social objectives.'

Colin Crooks wants 'to make a measurable difference to the way UK plc thinks about waste and resources' and would like to see social entrepreneurs 'spread the word into every corner of the UK and beyond that there is a new, dynamic way of doing business than can change lives, make things better and make money.'

Reed Paget, on the other hand, needs a break:

'Apart from a long holiday ... I intend to set up a clean energy company (and help put Exxon out of business) ... I hope that environmentalists and social activists around the world add another weapon to their arsenal: a profit and loss sheet. I believe that if such people were to launch a fleet of businesses that provide people with goods and services in a sustainable manner, the earth might have a future.'

But there are not enough social entrepreneurs to do this as yet. The world needs more of them. They generate ideas, boost innovation, encourage experimentation and help develop more viable long-term solutions to social and environmental problems. We need to get more social entrepreneurs coming forward because our times are crying out for it, as we'll see in the next chapter.

And we need to ensure that those who have embarked on the journey are properly supported and helped to develop to their full potential. More and more social entrepreneurs are undertaking training both on and off the job: some courses fit around their work commitments, others deliberately take them away to allow time to reflect (and sometimes to help them learn to delegate responsibility).

Social entrepreneurs are taking training and qualifications more seriously. Many are taking MBAs (and more MBA courses are teaching social entrepreneurship, not least Stanford University and the Oxford Said Business School). The support and ideas networks are growing; so are the number and professionalism of organisations dedicated to identifying those with potential and helping them to achieve it. Gradually the career paths and support structures we considered earlier will become better understood. All these factors will help bring forward new social entrepreneurs and keep them going once they have started.

To be sure, there is a long way to go. Some countries have fewer than one high-level social entrepreneur per million people; others are up to one in 100,000. It is encouraging that the UK is starting 1,000 new young social entrepreneurs a year through UnLtd, and perhaps the same again as a result of the higher level of activity in the field. To put the figures in context, though, as many as one in 10 people of working age run their own business, with as many as 374,000 new businesses started in 2007.[17]

Should we be aiming to have, say, one in 100 of the population operate as social entrepreneurs? What would this take? What would it look like? In this new world, business would be run as if people really mattered, some big businesses would make the transition to social enterprises, and success would be judged by social impact. Moreover, 'a millionaire will not just be someone who has made a million pounds but also someone who has changed a million lives.'[18] It's time to get *really* rich...

■ ■ ■

It's never too late or too early to start the journey into social entrepreneurship. Opportunities are growing fast: the citizen sector is expanding hugely.

We've looked at some groups – young people at school, students, business people, charity workers – who could be breeding grounds for future social entrepreneurs or valuable contributors to the development of more socially entrepreneurial approaches. But the list is far from comprehensive. As people search for greater meaning in their life and work, social entrepreneurship is well placed to be a career-defining concept. However, it's more a state of mind than a specific role. You can be socially entrepreneurial in a multitude of different contexts.

Ashoka's Bill Drayton believes that social entrepreneurship is opening up a new language, a new career possibility, a new category of activity, and new possibilities of self-realisation. 'A career in social entrepreneurship is quite magical. It offers huge impacts, a direct fit with your values, increasing public recognition and support, no glass ceilings.'[19]

What makes you follow the dream? Simply the dream itself. Maybe we shouldn't try to reduce it to a rational calculation of pros and cons. If you have the passion, follow it where it leads.

Pause for reflection and action

All of us, whether or not we belong to one of the groups in this chapter, can do something to become more aware of and involved in social entrepreneurship.

■ Look for the right first step that could move you a little way from where you are now to where you'd like to be. It might be volunteering, a training course, some reading or making contact with a particular person or organisation.
■ Most of us give to charity. Ask how your giving can be more effective. How about:
  ○ Clubbing together with others to create more meaningful chunks of money
  ○ Looking for organisations that seem to punch above their weight
  ○ Considering funding a specific project that shows potential – perhaps a pilot that could be expanded if successful.
■ At work, whether or not you are the boss, look for opportunities to create social impact. You could form a partnership with a third-sector organisation or set up a new project within your organisation to generate awareness and lead to bigger projects or a new way of doing things.

10

The big issues: Manifesto pledges for social entrepreneurs

'The supreme purpose of history is to build a better world.'
Herbert Hoover,
US president 1929–33

Think of the biggest, scariest, hairiest problems you can imagine, and I'll tell you how social entrepreneurs are tackling them all. I mean it: everything from homelessness to terrorism, the community playgroup to the global environment.

Social entrepreneurs are the people we should look to for the breakthroughs that we yearn for, the changes that will enable us to escape from the old vicious circles. This is one of the conclusions of a provocatively titled report by the SustainAbility think-tank and Skoll Foundation, 'Growing Opportunity: Entrepreneurial solutions to insoluble problems.'[1]

Delusion or visionary genius? You decide...

Climate change and the environment

We have already seen how Nic Frances is plotting to transform consumers' behaviour through his ambitious environmental businesses. How Tim Smit has created Eden as an educational and consciousness-raising tool to persuade people of the need for change and offer ways to achieve it. How Colin Crooks built a business on recycling and replicated it nationally. How Sir Richard Branson is investing billions in clean aircraft fuel technology.

Can strategies like these really address Al Gore's challenge to slow global warming by reducing CO_2 and other greenhouse emissions by more than the basic 5% reduction proposed in the Kyoto treaty? In late 2007, the United Nations declared that there is a scientific consensus that we have as little as ten years to do this.[2] The UK's Stern report argues that we need to spend 1% of global GDP now to prevent an economic loss of at least 5% of GDP in the future – a loss that would have a disproportionate impact on poorer countries. Global warming is an economic as well as an environmental issue with a business case for serious investment (and profit) now.

The preachers of doom lament that developing countries will continue to produce increasing quantities of CO_2 and that they can't be expected to suspend their development goals. That may be so, but it will be the socially motivated entrepreneurs who find a way to achieve sustainable development. Energy prices are rising. This is the era of the US$ 50–100 barrel of oil. What the world sees as a problem, the social entrepreneur sees as an opportunity: renewable energy technologies are becoming increasingly viable, and fossil fuels are dwindling and becoming unaffordable.

Social businessman Jeremy Leggett of Solar Century has a vision of solar panels and micro-generation replacing fossil fuels. Matt Scott of Cosmos Ignite has developed a solar-powered light for poor households in developing countries to replace polluting and health-threatening kerosene lamps – a neat innovation that kills two birds with one stone.

Solutions to our biggest environmental problems will have to come from a combination of political will, scientific progress and behavioural change. The social entrepreneur has a role in all of these: creating the impetus for and belief in change which in turn alters consumer behaviour one person at a time, so exerting pressure on politicians and leading businesses to new market-driven solutions. Since some two-fifths of greenhouse-gas emissions result directly from decisions taken by individuals, changes in personal behaviour can both make a direct impact and influence the corporate behaviour responsible for the majority of emissions.

Jeff Skoll's genius was to see how a film could be used to change the world's perception of the issue – and Al Gore's was to be the communicator.

Housing and homelessness

Housing a growing and divided world is proving to be another seemingly insuperable challenge.

- About 1 billion people are living in inadequate housing in urban areas alone.

- The UN estimated that one in three urban dwellers lived in poverty in 2007.
- About 100 million people worldwide are homeless.
- In Central Asian republics, half of the urban poor live in slum conditions.
- Of Poland's total housing stock of 11 million units, 1 million need major renovation and 300,000 should be demolished.
- Almost every building in Armenia is considered to fall below safety requirements for protection against earthquakes.[3]

Affluent societies are not without their problems either. Housing has become so unaffordable even for people on average incomes that it is creating another fracture in social relations between the haves and have-nots.

There is more to housing than bricks and mortar, as many failed public housing experiments over the years have proved. Good communities need social capital for real quality of life.

On the positive side, we can point to some excellent socially entrepreneurial responses. The founder of Habitat for Humanity, Millard Fuller, was a successful businessman who packed it all in to set up an organisation that has built over 200,000 low-cost housing units across the globe over the past 30 years. Abbé Pierre, the French monk who set up the worldwide network of Emmaus communities, was a visionary social entrepreneur. He designed a mini-economy that succeeds by combining the right level of incentives with appropriate housing and work. Tony McGann is the community social entrepreneur behind the Eldonian self-housing project in Liverpool that enabled local people to prevent their community being bulldozed and redesign it to their own specification.

Pete Cunningham has virtually eradicated homelessness from one English town, Southport on Merseyside, through a buy-to-let scheme with a blended social and financial return that allows people to feel good about investing in the property market by providing homeless people with somewhere to live. Could your community achieve something similar?

Grameen housing loans are giving Bangladeshi women the chance to improve the roofs over their families' heads. Somsook Boonyabancha is forging a new way to unlock urban slum housing that could have worldwide applications.

All of these initiatives are about far more than just buildings. Just as the problems are multi-faceted, so must be the solutions. Recall Vera Cordeiro's health scheme: one of the ways to help a post-operative child make a full recovery is to improve their living environment, and particularly their housing. Vera's team have tackled the challenge head on.

In Brazil, the culture of violence in the favelas (shanty towns) is a barrier to long-term improvement. So Gary Barker, the director of non-governmental organisation Instituto Promundo in Rio de Janeiro, has responded by going upstream to address the root causes of violence. His key innovation was to identify and work with community members who don't conform to established cultural norms such as male machismo. Through group classes, community campaigns, training and mentoring, Gary has found that he can significantly reduce serious violence in the favelas. He is now targeting parenting styles to prevent children from falling into common patterns of joining street gangs and trafficking in drugs.

Kate King was upset by the disengagement and anti-social behaviour of young people on her Sheffield council housing estate, so she set up the Dreamscheme project to create incentives for constructive behaviour. Young people can get involved in a range of activities such as volunteering for which they receive points towards rewards that they choose for themselves. King seems to have hit upon the right psychology: the project has gone on to engage hundreds of young people in 63 franchised locations around Britain, and now Uganda.[4]

Interlocking issues: employment, drugs, crime, health

There are a range of interconnecting issues that go to make up a good or bad community. You may have a home but if you don't have a job or a means of making a living it will quickly feel like a prison. If your community suffers from drug problems or anti-social behaviour you will suffer with it. Even wealth can't entirely insulate you from the problems: research shows that rich people in very unequal societies suffer a variety of stresses as a result.[5] So it is in everyone's interests to build better and fairer societies. Social entrepreneurs can be found at work on all the factors that create quality of life, often pursuing integrated responses.

The search for meaningful, properly rewarded work is a global challenge that connects marginalised people from developing countries with the workers, citizens and consumers of the brave new post-industrial world. Robert Roth was offended that even the thriving Swiss economy seemed unable to create enough opportunities for its young people, so he established the Job Factory in Basle to take unemployed young people who would otherwise be on welfare schemes and provide them with training in a range of professions from e-commerce to guitar making. The work that the young people do is as close to market reality as possible, and the enterprise survives only if it trades successfully. Craig Dearden-Phillips built a social enterprise called Speaking Up that focuses on advocacy for those with a disability or learning difficulty so that they are no longer passive recipients of social care but active shapers of their own lives.

David Robinson and Andrew (Lord) Mawson have created multi-faceted community initiatives in the toughest parts of East London. Mawson's Bromley-by-Bow Centre offers an integrated medical centre, business units, church and arts projects where your doctor is as likely to prescribe art therapy as drugs for some conditions. The lessons from such pioneering work have been spread nationally through healthy living centres that take a holistic view of what makes people well. Yet all this had unpromising beginnings in a run-down, poorly attended church where Mawson arrived as the new minister in the mid-1980s. His remarkable success seems to have stemmed from his willingness to say 'yes' to people with any idea at all, no matter how small or bizarre, and then to see where the idea took them together. Many of the people involved had spent most of their lives being told 'no,' so Mawson's receptiveness triggered a transformation that led to real socially entrepreneurial community development.[6]

Terrorism

At first sight it may seem hopelessly optimistic to imagine that even the most innovative approaches could hope to tackle the roots of terrorism. But is it conceivable that by building positive international relationships across many divides we could begin to heal the inequalities, resentments and cultural conflict that fuel extremism?

Sure enough, social entrepreneurs are at work on the problem at a variety of levels. At the grass roots there are people like Dirk Paterson, who founded City Gateway to create employment and business opportunities for disadvantaged young people in Spitalfields, right next to the financial nerve centre of the City of London. Many of them are young Muslims disillusioned with the lack of opportunity available to them. Social enterprise is being used here as an economic tool and to foster a sense of social and cultural integration.

Yunus won a Nobel prize for the contribution he and Grameen Bank have made to peace because the award committee recognised that tackling poverty and alienation reduces the underlying causes of conflict. We have to hope that Roshaneh Zafar's similar microcredit work in Pakistan and Sakena Yacoobi's educational work in Afghanistan will contribute to a more stable and prosperous situation in their respective countries. Victoria Hale's health work may just change perceptions of the nations that have created the pharmaceutical giants.

The mega-social entrepreneurs we looked at in chapter 5 are using their networks to extend the hand of friendship across the globe and show that western countries can have entirely peaceful and positive intentions and want to see every nation flourish with a development path of its own choosing.

But if we keep on asking 'why?' all the problems ultimately point back to one thing ...

Poverty

Most of the serious social problems we face as a planet are connected to poverty as a cause, contributory factor or effect.

Over 1 billion of the world's people live on less than US$1 a day and more than half the population – 4 billion – on less than US$2 a day.[7] People below the poverty line are more vulnerable to starvation, disease, war and natural disaster.

Social entrepreneurs have a key role to play, as these contrasting approaches suggest.

Bunker Roy is an Indian doctor who was spurred into action by a famine in his home state, which prompted him to establish the Barefoot College. This innovative rural education network has trained two generations of villagers with no formal qualifications to become healthcare workers, solar engineers, hand-pump mechanics and teachers in their communities. Rural youths once regarded as unemployable now install and maintain solar electricity systems, hand pumps and tanks for drinking water. Over 100,000 people in 110 villages now have access to safe drinking water, education, health and employment. The scheme also reduces the tendency for rural people to migrate to the cities that Roy believes is encouraged by the formal education system.

Nicholas Negroponte is a professor of media technology at MIT who has set up a non-profit initiative called One Laptop Per Child. Its vision is to get a US$100 laptop into the hands of as many children in the developing world as possible as a tool for education and development. Designed to be simple and robust enough to work in tough rural environments, the colourful and funky-looking machines are highly popular. In a stroke of marketing genius, Negroponte is offering 'one for the price of two' to US purchasers who get one machine for themselves and pay for another to be sent abroad.[8]

Different starting points, different solutions. Economist C. K. Prahalad has written about 'the fortune at the bottom of the pyramid': if products and services can be designed to meet the needs and pockets of the poorest tiers of the world's population, there is money to be made.[9] Social entrepreneurs are ideally placed to be among these innovators. Matt Scott's affordable lighting system can pay for itself within six to nine months of replacing kerosene, but the poorest people can't afford to make the initial investment. Enter microcredit, which has made such tiny loans possible.

Tackling poverty is about getting a very large number of very small changes to take place and designing systems that work with human nature rather than against the grain of it. As Muhammad Yunus observes,

> 'Things are going wrong not because of "market failure". It is much deeper than that. Let us be brave and admit that it is because of "conceptualisation failure." More specifically, it is the failure to capture the essence of a human being in our theory. Everyday human beings are not one-dimensional entities, they are excitingly multi-dimensional and indeed very colourful.'[10]

One example of multiple small changes in action across a wide front can be seen in the work of the Fair Trade entrepreneurs who make meaningful trading relationships possible and create market pressure on other traders to change their behaviour. Their messages are being taken up by the entrepreneurial campaigning community to demand reform of international trade rules so that poorer countries can trade their way to a better future.

Rethinking human need

Muhammad Yunus has a huge overarching vision: the wholesale eradication of poverty from the world. He sees Grameen as 'a message of hope, a programme for putting homelessness and destitution in a museum so that one day our children will visit it and ask how we could have allowed such a terrible thing to go on for so long.'[11]

As I write, the effects of the global credit crunch are still unfolding. No one can yet predict the extent of the havoc it will wreak. Banks have been convulsed in a perfect storm of bad lending decisions wrapped up in ultra-complex financial instruments devised with profit rather than people in view. Detached from real communities, flows of capital sweep the world, and when they go wrong, they go badly wrong. If ever there was a time to learn from the likes of Grameen, where the ratio of savers to borrowers is sufficient to ride out the storm, this is it. If ever there was a time to hold up our hands and say we have failed to understand what is really going on, this is it. In short, it's time to let the social entrepreneurs take over.

In effect, Yunus is posing a big question. Do we genuinely believe that the world will get better if we continue on our present course: pursuing maximum profit and growth at almost any cost with no more than a light government hand on the regulation of markets to prevent scandals like Enron, plus sufficient largesse in the form of corporate social responsibility and individual charitable giving to make a conscience-salving gesture at tackling some of the worst manifestations of poverty? As he says, 'poor people are not asking for charity, because charity is not a solution for poverty.'[12]

The challenge is twofold: the quantitative task of scaling up, and the qualitative task of cultural change.

Pierre Omidyar of eBay asked how much it would cost to take microcredit to the whole world and calculated that around US$50-60 billion should do the trick. As he points out, that's a lot of money if it has to come from charitable foundations, but private capital could deliver it. Look at it that way, he says, and '$60 billion is nothing.'[13]

When Omidyar saw the high success rates of microcredit at getting people permanently out of poverty and the low default rate on small business loans, he realised that here was a viable business opportunity. So his Omidyar Network is committing most of its money and energy to commercialising microfinance by turning it into a mainstream investing opportunity. Omidyar gave US$100 million to the investment office at Tufts University, his *alma mater*, on condition that money managers invest exclusively in for-profit microfinance institutions. But his strategy extends further than this, so he is also funding academic research and is about to begin lobbying foreign governments to reform local banking regulations so that microfinance outfits will have an easier time attracting global capital. 'I don't believe that there is a for-profit answer to everything,' he admits, but 'the largest impact we can have with this wealth will be testing a theory that business can be a tool for good.'[14]

It's imperative that we find and nurture social entrepreneurs who are able to nudge humanity's largest institutions — corporations and governments — into a more socially entrepreneurial direction. This is the way that social entrepreneurship will make the jump from distinct socially enterprising projects, however big, to influencing the mainstream. Imagine the major international banks doing microcredit — properly. Imagine the multinational food and drink giants competing with each other to deliver a stronger social impact — because their customers demand it. Imagine the big-league drugs companies finding ways to drive profitability from eradicating preventable disease.

How could all this be possible?

Conditions for growth

To achieve this potential we need to help existing social entrepreneurs scale up, and future social entrepreneurs develop faster and more effectively.

This requires a set of financial innovations, a truly global support network, and cultural changes in the way social entrepreneurs are regarded and nurtured.

Financial

Among social entrepreneurs, resource constraints are the most frequently cited source of frustration and lack of progress. What solutions do they need?

1. Start-up funds: anyone with a good idea needs to be able to tap into support and funding. A good example of seed or starter funding is the UnLtd model in the UK and now India, which is designed to make it relatively easy to access initial support.
2. Growth funds: flexible financing mechanisms for second-stage operations available for social entrepreneurs who are ready to expand or copy their initial projects.
3. Major replication to enable wide franchising or scaling up. Only a handful of financial institutions provide significant later-stage capital to models with high potential for replication and scalability. Other possibilities to generate the volume of funding required might include:

    ■ Social venture capitalists who are beginning to apply business approaches and financial mechanisms to significant social projects. Skoll Foundation's chief operating officer, Richard Fahey, sums up the new thinking when he says 'We have the view that our capital is a continuum' that can be used for higher or lower returns depending on the situation. Governments can help too: for instance, the UK government is examining ways of putting unclaimed bank accounts to use to fund social investment.

    ■ A social stock market where socially minded investors could trade shares whose value is linked to the financial and/or social impacts of social enterprises, with the aim of getting capital flowing to institutions that can demonstrate they will deliver. Competition is healthy: there are several microcredit organisations in Bangladesh, for instance, so Grameen doesn't have a monopoly. Social stock exchanges will encourage capital to move to more efficient and effective organisations.

    ■ Special-purpose funds and prizes to encourage innovation in particular fields or in response to crises. Yunus proposes the setting up of a social business innovation fund ready to target social entrepreneurs who will rebuild communities after disasters. Competitions such as the X-Prize, a prestigious and valuable American award best known for its space-flight challenges, are now offering prizes for the most promising interventions in poverty and education.

Klaus Schwab observes that the microcredit industry took 20 years to grow: 'We want to shorten that timespan in future.'[15] Schwab is supporting the Global Exchange for Social Investment (GEXSI); other exchanges include Altruistiq and EthEx. Such institutions should allow individual investors with ethical as well as financial criteria to participate in the financing of world-changing companies.

Support networks

Ashoka has demonstrated the benefits of networking among social entrepreneurs, first to overcome their isolation and second to share ideas and experiences.

Many of the problems they encounter are much the same no matter where they operate. Ashoka is looking for ways to speed up the adoption and adaptation of the best solutions across boundaries and cultures. It calls this process 'blueprint copying.'

Another level of networking being promoted by Ashoka and Schwab is between social entrepreneurs and commercial business entrepreneurs seeking to develop a common agenda and meaningful partnerships. Skoll's annual World Forum pulls together hundreds of social entrepreneurs at various stages to share ideas and be inspired. The web is another key part of the picture, with networks such as i-genius, UnLtd World and Skoll's Social Edge forum.

These virtual and real linkages are creating a web of relationships and trust between those who are working for a better future. Our ambition should be to promote the development of a fully global and cooperative process for seeking out and nurturing social entrepreneurs.

A mass movement online

Social entrepreneurs are harnessing the power of the internet to spread the message to a wider audience and engage more people in social entrepreneurship.

In one pilot initiative, the Bebo social networking site worked with UnLtd, the foundation for social entrepreneurs, with the aim of using the phenomenon of online social networking as an agent for positive social change. Bebo users – who number over 30 million worldwide – could select projects each month that they felt deserved financial support. From this list, a panel of experts from both organisations drew up a shortlist of projects with the

contd.

greatest potential to make a positive impact on society. Finally, the entire Bebo community voted for their favourite project. The one with the most votes each month won a financial award and ongoing support from UnLtd to get started.

The idea was to give Bebo's networks of creative, socially conscious people a mechanism to turn their ideas into reality. Cliff Prior of UnLtd commented: 'Social entrepreneurship is fast becoming a dynamic movement which is increasingly harnessing the internet's potential. It's not hard to see that this is where the future of social entrepreneurship lies.'

Another initiative, Missionfish, makes it possible to link your sale on eBay to a contribution to charity.[16] Nick Aldridge, CEO of Missionfish, explains: 'Online networks and business models provide an exciting channel for bringing social enterprise to the masses. Our first goal, building on a global partnership with eBay, will be to turn individual eBay sellers into mini social enterprises.'

Cultural

There is still a long way to go in every country in terms of gaining recognition for social entrepreneurship, let alone credibility among institutions and the public at large. According to Pamela Hartigan of the Schwab Foundation, legitimacy and credibility are often lacking because social entrepreneurs usually challenge the accepted way of doing things.[17] This may be because they need to take on vested interests, but there is also a certain amount of suspicion and misunderstanding of the social entrepreneur's role and intentions. Some countries have cultural barriers to entrepreneurship in general, or specifically where women are concerned. 'You're not crazy, you're just a social entrepreneur' was one helpful comment noted by Vera Cordeiro of Renascer in Brazil, who had been suffering self-doubt and some derision from traditionalist medical colleagues.

So what might contribute to cultural change?

- Better training at all levels: school, higher education, business school
- More young people choosing to be social entrepreneurs
- Incorporation of social enterprise into the school curriculum
- Good role models
- Parental understanding and empathy
- Knowledge of available career paths
- Proactive enabling measures from government to build a culture of social entrepreneurship that involves genuine delegation of responsibility (particularly for public services) without loss of control (and not purely for the sake of saving money)

- More coverage of social entrepreneurship in the media, as in the films produced by Participant Productions for the Skoll Foundation and for public broadcast in the US
- Certification mechanisms like those pioneered by the Fair Trade movement: there is now a Social Enterprise Mark being developed in the UK
- Incorporation of social entrepreneurship into economic theory and business models so that it is taught and debated at all levels of business education.

As initiatives develop and those who work on them gain support, funding and a higher profile, the culture will gradually shift. Young people will then be inspired, businesses challenged as to how they can help, and politicians and governments convinced of the benefits of promoting wider participation in social entrepreneurship.

All pull together

It is now possible to see how the various strands of work by many different social entrepreneurs could come together:

- The structural change social entrepreneurs such as Bob Geldof and Bono who campaign, lobby and demonstrate how to make trade fairer.
- The Fair Trade social entrepreneurs on the ground such as Richard Adams and Penny Newman who create routes to market and establish proper rewards for the producers.
- The microcredit social entrepreneurs such as Muhammad Yunus and Fazle Abed who provide the means by which producers can raise their output, improve their housing and care for their families.
- The community-based social entrepreneurs like Andrew Mawson and Eric Samuels who are making people's lives better in a million different small but sustainable ways.
- The social business entrepreneurs who invent new ways of combining social, environmental and financial value, such as Tim Smit and Nic Frances.
- And all the social entrepreneurs who enter mainstream business and turn established models upside down ...

Lessons for business

Social entrepreneurs are not just demonstrating that there is a better way of doing social and economic development; they are also demonstrating that there is a better way of doing business. Indeed, business is starting to draw a range of lessons from the activities of social entrepreneurs.

Creative and innovative thinking

The core skill exhibited by social entrepreneurs is the ability to design and implement radically new solutions. If necessity is the mother of invention, the way that social entrepreneurs deploy limited resources to tackle the most serious of challenges provides insights for any business or organisation wanting to achieve more with less.

Daniel Pink, author of *A Whole New Mind*,[18] believes that we have now passed through the Knowledge Age into a Conceptual Age that will place value on more inventive and empathetic thinking. Business leaders in Australia have observed that social entrepreneurs are at the cutting edge of this development: 'There's a lot of talk now around what's called "the whole-minded aptitude,"' says Jan Owen of Social Venture Australia. 'How do you look for the white space? What's the relationship between relationships? These are skills of not-for-profit people, particularly those who have been working in very difficult, crisis-driven situations. They have to develop complex problem-solving skills in the most unlikely situations, and they have the freedom and capacity to innovate.'[19] It's about more than just thinking outside the box, according to Sir Geoffrey Chandler of Sustain-Ability; it's about 'breaking the box open.'[20]

This is the only way to face up to the toughest problems besetting policymakers: those complex and multi-faceted issues that defy all conventional interventions. No money, no credit; no credit, no money. No home, no job; no job ...

Yet social entrepreneurs are not deterred. Jack Sim is squaring up to the challenge of bringing sanitation to the world, a challenge where a huge logistical problem is exacerbated by its status as a cultural taboo. Muhammad Yunus speaks of the need for 'reconceptualisation': unblocking an issue by looking at it in a new way. We saw how Colin Crooks approaches the problem of seeing both furniture and unemployed people consigned to the scrapheap; in his words, 'all waste is really a resource in the wrong place and . . . everyone no matter how marginalised can make a positive contribution at work and in society if given the chance.'

We need to find ways to enable all these people to give full expression to their ideas and their energy.

Opening new markets, creating new sources of value

In the long run, believes analyst Charlie Leadbeater, social entrepreneurs may have their biggest impact by being 'disruptive innovators' and opening up markets that bigger organisations simply can't see, such as the Fair Trade movement.[21] Corporations working on their own may not be able to capture these opportunities, but they can in partnership with social businesses. A good example is French dairy company Danone's partnership with Grameen to supply fortified yoghurt products to the undernourished people of Bangladesh. What began with a simple handshake between Muhammad Yunus and Danone's chairman Franck Riboud has led to a business opportunity that would not otherwise have existed. Though the business model envisages that the project will break even rather than turn a profit, Danone reaps the benefit of establishing a positive reputation for its brand and a market platform for future products.[22]

Jeff Skoll's Participant Productions has built a brand and a business model tailored to the existing niche market of the serious film. By making such films attractive to invest in, Participant has increased their chances of being seen by a wider audience – and it has done so by an unexpected means: a social campaign that runs alongside each film and raises awareness of it. The campaign for *An Inconvenient Truth* was so effective that advance ticket sales made it the most profitable film per screening for a couple of weekends after its opening.[23]

Customers are attracted to a good product wedded to a sincere mission, as Anita Roddick proved twenty or thirty years ago with the Body Shop.

These examples show different ways of connecting with contrasting markets: ethical consumers in affluent nations and marginalised consumers in poorer ones. People are more than consumers, but here are businesses that really want to connect with them, and to make a difference.

In their book *The Power of Unreasonable People*, John Elkington and Pamela Hartigan identify ten markets they think are especially suited to social entrepreneurship, ranging from ageing, health, gender-based and nutrition-related demand through financial and educational markets, digital and security opportunities to the universal challenges of environment and resources.[24] These will be the areas that social entrepreneurs should be particularly busy in; perhaps you can think of ideas that might meet some of these needs. This is why social outcomes are so valuable, in both senses of the word: blended value may be a source of competitive advantage for innovative companies, and social businesses can actually create value of their own.

Harnessing staff motivation

Social entrepreneurship is starting to change the game for companies keen to recruit and retain the best people. Young, highly educated and ambitious young people are increasingly asking in job interviews what level of community involvement big corporations can offer, according to Julie White of major Australian bank Macquarie. Gib Bulloch's experience at Accenture shows how staff morale and retention can be boosted by corporate engagement that goes beyond the regular team-building mode of corporate volunteering.

Partnership with a social enterprise can provide that experience. When business people mentor social entrepreneurs, they can impart valuable wisdom. But the benefits flow in both directions: they get to learn about 'whole-minded' problem-solving approaches in a challenging environment that has lessons for any business that wants to listen.

Leadership is one area in which social entrepreneurs are ahead of the pack. 'Social entrepreneurs have exceptional qualities because they are driven and deeply passionate about their work,' says Jan Owen of Social Venture Australia. 'They don't do it because they want to build an organisation to become a manager or leader, but because they want to create change; and with that unbridled passion comes the ability to motivate and bring others. Millions of dollars are being spent in training people in the commercial area to have the skills that social entrepreneurs naturally bring.'[25]

It's all about harnessing human motivation to get involved in the organisations that are making a genuine difference, and to put in your best effort when you are there. Staff from Danone have reported the satisfaction that their involvement in the Grameen partnership has brought them: as its managing director exclaimed, 'We'll never thank you enough for bringing meaning to our business life.'[26]

And the outcome can be as productive as the process: as a commentator on Jeff Skoll's Participant Productions observed, 'When you give outstanding people the chance to work on something they care passionately about, often you get a great result.'[27]

A whole new business model

If the founder of the World Economic Forum at Davos thinks something is important, we would all do well to take note. Klaus Schwab calls social entrepreneurship a new paradigm.[28] Is it what the business world is looking for: the reconciliation of ethics and economics, markets and meaning, profits and purpose?

Social business entrepreneurs are doing business in their own right, but the way they are doing it is changing the terrain on which all businesses compete. If in future big businesses have to compete with social entrepreneurs and each other to demonstrate ethical credentials and social impact, then a small rudder will be beginning to steer a very big ship in a more constructive direction. Muhammad Yunus calls social business 'the missing piece of the capitalist system' and envisages it changing not just the response to social problems but the culture of commercial firms and indeed capitalism itself.[29]

To paraphrase Bill Clinton, it's the *social* economy, stupid. And it's about building a better world.

■ ■ ■

Our profile of the social entrepreneur is complete. These are the new business people of the twenty-first century. They have insights into innovative and effective ways to tackle the most difficult problems our planet faces. They operate in a range of arenas, creating social businesses, pro-social commercial businesses and citizen-sector initiatives all of which influence the practice of mainstream business and policymaking. And they are influencing business behaviour through example, partnership, pressure and leadership.

There are telling signs that social entrepreneurship is about to take off, with interest from governments, major funders and business leaders who are not only speaking the language but living it. The practice of social entrepreneurship is growing in most countries and the subject is becoming a field of academic study. Our aim should be to do more social entrepreneurship, encourage it all levels and find ways to realise the full potential of the pioneering ideas that show the greatest promise.

There will be those who argue that if capitalism is the cause of so many of the world's problems, business can't be expected to find the solutions. Or that a few social entrepreneurs can't possibly solve intractable problems that have refused to yield to decades of effort by governments, big business and the third sector. But this is a counsel of despair. We have grounds for hope. Peace prizes are going to those who are preventing future conflicts. Climate change activists are using the only weapon that operates at sufficient scale and speed: business. Pernicious diseases are being eradicated.

Doing nothing is not an option. Michael Norton, founder of Youthbank, comments that the biggest challenge is not the problems themselves, but apathy. Instead of shrugging in resignation or asking 'What if anything can we do about this terrible problem?' we should be asking 'What are the biggest opportunities for social entrepreneurs to meet these needs?'

Pause for reflection and action

We've concentrated on a few big issues in this chapter. Here are a few more (and you'll think of others). Over to you! Can you see chances to get involved with any of them?

- Biofuels and balancing them with food production
- Care of the elderly
- Child obesity and welfare
- Doorstep debt and predatory lenders
- Seasonal employment in coastal areas
- Rural employment
- Public-service delivery
- Transport, congestion and pollution
- Leisure.

11

A vision: transforming the personal and the planet

'What I would say, as an old man of the twentieth century, to you people of the twenty-first century, is 'Go for it! Don't be put off! Be persistent, persistent, persistent!' I don't think the next century will be any different: the resistance to new ideas will be much the same – and the means to overcoming it will be the same. You will need all the guile you can muster and all the persistence. Don't dismiss all your good ideas if they don't seem good ideas to your friends and other people. Believe in yourself. Go for it.'

The late Lord Michael Young speaking at a social entrepreneurs' conference, December 1999

W e've now completed our tour of the landscape of social entrepreneurship. In the process we have met a few of the tremendous range of social entrepreneurs who are getting on with the job of building a better world on the ground, piece by piece, in virtually every country. A multitude of different people, of all races, backgrounds and ages, are out there tackling a spectrum of social, economic and environmental issues. And doing so in a way that not only bridges the old divides of public, private and third sector but also colonises these sectors, changing them from within.

A handful are operating at a stratospheric level where they can see the threads of all this activity, all this potential, and are pulling them together, weaving them into a new pattern: a social entrepreneurship movement that spans the globe. Instead of being isolated and often misunderstood individuals, participants are now organised, supported and able to play their part in a bigger picture: the creation of a new social fabric.

Some of their ideas are local but important; others already have national or international scope. They share a common goal: to breathe new life into old challenges by adopting the principles of a businesslike approach: leverage, income generation, mass-market adoption. It's a new sustainable and flexible way of doing business, and a new *meaning* for doing business.

These are all driven, visionary entrepreneurs who put their skills to use in the service of social change. And they all have the potential to change established patterns and models. Chances are, someone somewhere is already working on the next idea that will go global.

What does this mean for you and me as individuals? And for the whole growing group of social entrepreneurs as a mass movement? *Everyone* can be more socially entrepreneurial. There may not be any recognisable career path yet, but it's a choice that will lead you into hugely exciting work opportunities and life experiences.

Global challenges at every scale are getting greater, not fewer, so we need more and more social entrepreneurship in every country. To achieve the cultural change that will unleash a greater volume and quality of socially entrepreneurial activity on society, we need the institutions of government, business and society to understand and support social entrepreneurs more effectively.

We need more social entrepreneurs in order to help the movement grow faster and attain critical mass, so that it can achieve:

■ More impact
■ More experimentation leading to more discoveries that may help tackle 'insoluble' problems
■ Recognition as a valid business sector in its own right with large numbers and a wide diversity of practitioners.

And we need socially entrepreneurial organisations and places too:

■ Third-sector organisations
■ Business entrepreneurs and their companies
■ Communities.

We all need to maximise our potential not just for the collective good, but also for our own sake.

What you are capable of becoming

As you will have gathered by now, I firmly believe that *anyone* can become more socially entrepreneurial. You can get more out of the money you give, your volunteering, your working life. You can make an incremental step or a complete career change. Every human being has the potential within them to do good. We just need to find the opportunity to express it. Stuff gets in the way.

Those we have seen who managed to move beyond the reasons not to do something have found a new level of personal satisfaction. The fulfilment that comes from helping others to realise their potential or overcome basic life-restricting obstacles can be greater than anything most of us experience in our conventional working lives.

We may be witnessing the start of a revolution. Talented young people who make money quickly early in their careers are looking for something meaningful, enduring and even world-changing to do with their cash and abilities in their next stage of life. Business people are moving into delivering social change as the bottom line. Old hands are finding new ways to use valuable experience instead of retiring into an unproductive twilight.

I hope that you, like me, have been inspired by the dreams, ambitions and achievements of the social entrepreneurs we have met in this book, and by the many other examples of great social entrepreneurs around the world. Could you follow your dreams in the same way? If you have the passion to solve a social challenge, your Excalibur moment could be just around the corner. Once you take hold of that sword and start addressing that need, your power as a social entrepreneur will grow. Even if you don't feel you can go that far, you can still be the supporter or enabler of other social entrepreneurs, or get involved in social enterprise in other ways.

To quote Jack Sim, social entrepreneurship has to become a way of life for businesses and for us as individuals.

Together everyone achieves more

Just as Eugenie Harvey's We Are What We Do movement sets out to improve the world through many small actions, lots of small social entrepreneurs will generate a whole lot of good, and some will become giant social entrepreneurs in their own right. The former director of the UK government's Social Enterprise Unit, Barbara Phillips, sees it like this:

> 'Don't discount the little 'uns: their total actually adds up to an awful lot of social action ... They will, together, raise the aspirations and quality of life for very, very many people. That, not size, is what really matters.'

But

'Who can say for sure which of today's "mad ideas" or "ordinary" local initiatives will be tomorrow's respected high-flyers and big-hitters?'[1]

Making a difference in local communities. Taking on the delivery of major parts of public services. Running big companies. Changing the world?

Start small. Stay small. Or grow. It doesn't matter. What does is starting, and trying.

We need more social entrepreneurs coming forward – greater numbers – and more social entrepreneurs scaling up – greater impact per person. Bill Drayton believes we should aim to have 5% of the population directly practising social entrepreneurship, which he thinks would change the whole culture.

For this to happen, it will be essential to make the case for the impact we can expect to see. But what is the impact of a social entrepreneur? Let's look at the UK. The School for Social Entrepreneurs has found that:

- 91% of SSE graduates go on to create jobs; 10% create more than 20 jobs
- 61% of graduates mobilise volunteers
- 82% of organisations established in the 1998 training intake are still operating, compared with the general business survival rate of 39% after eight years.[2]

Imagine these impacts multiplied worldwide! Microcredit started with Muhammad Yunus's US$27 personal loan; thirty years later it is a US$9 billion market. Ashoka selects individuals who are capable of massive change: the Yunuses of the future. Liam Black and Jeremy Nicholls challenge us to raise our sights to the Millennium Development Goals – the targets set by the UN for reducing poverty in the developing world by 2015 – and speak of a battle between 'the immovable object of global injustice defended by vested interests and the irresistible force of the growing movement of social entrepreneurs.'[3] There is a long way to go, but we have cause for hope. Another survey indicates that of over 70 social entrepreneurs surveyed, 68% are contributing to Millennium Development Goals.[4]

Social entrepreneurship is creating a new global dynamic. Bangladesh teaches the west about social capital. Idealistic young westerners set up businesses that tackle the inequitable legacies of colonialism. Fair Trade rewrites the rules in partnership across the continents. It's not a one-way street. We all stand to gain. And the problem that truly unites us all – climate change – can be addressed only if we work together.

When social enterprise becomes not so much a concept as an attitude or state of mind, the agenda for the socially enterprising becomes more exciting, especially where social entrepreneurs and private businesses begin to converse and collaborate. We need to be as creative as the big brands, many of which began life as upstarts challenging long-established multinational behemoths. Like them, social entrepreneurs question the established order and find ways to break the mould:

> 'By reconsidering how market needs are best met and who the consumers are — and might be — and by being transparent and accountable while rebooting the process of value creation, these people are set to have a profound impact on the world's most complex societal and environmental challenges. Their impact may be limited by their current scale, but could be limitless with the right business partners. We see this as the next wave of change.'[5]

When one in ten or one in five of the businesses in leading countries are run by social entrepreneurs; when every school pupil hears about the career options open to them if they pursue the social entrepreneur path; when every country has a thriving social business sector and begins to link up with others across the globe for fair trade and environmental protection; then the structures that have bound us will have to change. Our young social entrepreneurs are already demanding change and will soon be in positions of power to bring it about. Our consumer culture will demand more ethical products, whether local or international, that are produced in a way that contributes to the well-being of the producers and their communities.

Capitalism may have triumphed as the world's dominant economic system but it still faces serious challenges from within and without. If the question is no longer 'Can there be a socialist revolution?' but rather 'How can we make capitalism more humane?' the search for answers should occupy everyone in business and government. As Bill Gates recently said:

> 'If we can find approaches that meet the needs of the poor that generate profit for business and votes for politicians we will have found a sustainable way to reduce inequality in the world.'[6]

There are two ways for this to be realised. The first is to scale up true social businesses as a direct alternative to commercial businesses. As Muhammad Yunus says:

> 'The more sustainable social entrepreneurs there are, the more powerful they become as a business community. The future of the world lies in the hands of these

market-based social entrepreneurs. We cannot combat poverty within the ortho-
doxy of capitalism practiced today. Economic theory has not provided us with any
alternative to this familiar model but I argue that we can create a powerful alter-
native: a social-consciousness-driven private sector, created by social entrepre-
neurs.[7]

The second route is to achieve maximum leverage through partnerships and influence with mainstream business. The sectors are moving closer together and starting to look more like each other. Some of the world's largest businesses are keen to form partnerships with social entrepreneurs because, as one of them says,

'Social entrepreneurs are one potential wellspring of insight and inspiration.
Individuals from Bonn to Bangalore are seizing the chance to turn challenge into
opportunity, in the process pioneering new markets.... Our hope is that collabo-
rating with creative thinkers will help our people realise their full potential –
and better serve the needs of present and future customers.'[8]

Social enterprises can also be more nimble in responding to issues, and more welcomed by funders such as governments, than large corporations working alone. So partnering may enable big businesses to participate in a market they would otherwise not find easy to access. This prospect may set alarm bells ringing for those who fear the possible corruption of social goals by profit-hungry corporations. But they should bear in mind the opportunities for social entrepreneurs to influence the corporations. Bill Drayton believes that by:

'putting together new production and distribution chains that draw on the
unique strengths of business and social institutions at different points in the
production system, we can demonstrate enormous new markets and profit poten-
tial for business, very major new revenue flows for citizen groups and better, and
better-priced, products and services for everyone ... The financial pages and busi-
ness schools and management-consulting firms will be all over the idea. Not to
mention the business and social competitors of the pioneers! It is precisely this
sort of self-multiplication of an idea that is every entrepreneur's dream.'[9]

The convergence of markets and social principles will lead to a new kind of corporation according to Pamela Hartigan.[10] And for Muhammad Yunus, these new corporations will be in the vanguard of the new capitalism. The future will be about convergence: money flowing to the best solutions; the best solutions operating the best business models; the best business models being socially entrepreneurial.

Social entrepreneurship will move from being a subset of the third sector:

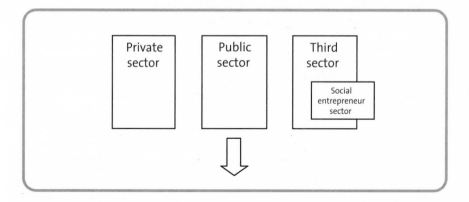

to being the glue that binds the different sectors together, and an approach that operators in each sector can adopt. It becomes the foundation for all sectors:

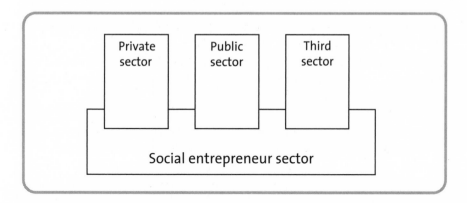

So what must we do?

Every generation has its blind spots: slavery, colonialism, racial segregation, individualism, conspicuous consumption. Each of these has been used to justify a particular economic and business model. What is our generation's blind spot? We have to hope that one day we will not be accused of having it within our power to end poverty and prevent environmental disaster, but failing to do so. What a devastating indictment if we knew the potential of social entrepreneurship, properly supported, but did not use it.

So we need to invest and organise effectively to maximise the potential and the impact of these change makers. We know what we have to do:

■ Devise reliable and widely understood systems for identifying and supporting those with the potential to become social entrepreneurs
■ Develop career options that work for a variety of social entrepreneurs
■ Find ways to provide appropriate funding at all levels
■ Value our social entrepreneurs
■ Persuade politicians to recognise that well-managed change can win popular support.

One day, the first decade of the twenty-first century could be celebrated as the era that spawned the social entrepreneur. New ways of thinking. New business models. New career opportunities. It's a whole new world. It's a revolution. To those who see it, and those who are about to find out, the future belongs to the social entrepreneur.

Appendix of resources

Courses for adults

Skoll Centre for Social Entrepreneurship, Said Business School, Oxford University
Promotes social entrepreneurship worldwide by sponsoring the annual Skoll World Forum on Social Entrepreneurship, conducting research, and providing fellowships for MBA students specialising in social entrepreneurship. Runs Launchpad, an initiative to find responses to pressing needs. www.sbs.ox.ac.uk/skoll

University of East London
MA, Postgraduate Diploma, Certificate in Social Enterprise: qualifications developed with Social Enterprise London. www.uel.ac.uk/cis/courses/postgrad.htm

University of Cambridge
The Master of Studies (M.St.) in Social Enterprise and Community Development is a two-year, part-time degree at the Institute of Continuing Education and the Judge Business School. www.cont-ed.cam.ac.uk

School for Social Entrepreneurs, London
Year-long part-time (one day a week) programmes for people starting or building social enterprises. www.sse.org.uk

Anglia Ruskin University
Runs *3rd Sector Futures* initiative; ask about their archive of past materials including the 'Working in Social Enterprise' (WISE) course and other short courses such as Refresh Yourself (short uplifting sessions to bounce ideas off fellow social entrepreneurs). www.3rdsectorfutures.co.uk

Initiative on Social Enterprise, Harvard Business School, US
Promoting excellence in the leadership of social, public and business enterprise. www.hbs.edu/socialenterprise

Center for Social Innovation, Stanford University, US
University centre promoting the application of entrepreneurial management to the social sector. www.gsb.stanford.edu/csi

The University Network for Social Entrepreneurship
A virtual network that works with academics, researchers, practitioners and students to develop social entrepreneurship as a vocation and carry its principles into other disciplines and sectors. Designed as a resource hub and discussion forum to expand social entrepreneurship education and participation across the world. www.universitynetwork.org

Young people at school

Better World Heroes
Website for children to help inspire and educate them about people who have contributed to a better world. www.betterworldheroes.com

Social Enterprise At Schools (SEAS)
School programmes and web materials that guide you through enterprises such as setting up a café or jewellery business. www.seas-online.org.uk

Mark Your Mark
Organisation that helps young people make their ideas happen; has a strong social dimension: www.makeyourmark.org.uk

Young Enterprise / Junior Achievement
Programmes in over 100 countries around the world reaching nearly 7 million students each year. www.young-enterprise.org.uk; www.ja.org

Ethical Careers Guide
Website and book dedicated to broadening career decision-making. www.ethicalcareers.org

Working For A Charity
Promotes voluntary sector as a career option and provides information and training in managing volunteers and community organisations. www.wfac.org.uk

Volunteering

Social Entrepreneur Corps
International internship and volunteering programmes offering university students and recent graduates the chance to work at a grassroots level with professional social entrepreneurs. www.socialentrepreneurcorps.com

Timebank
National volunteering campaign raising awareness of giving time through voluntary work. www.timebank.org.uk

Online training and learning

Online learning modules for social enterprise
Free packages on social enterprise and social entrepreneurs.
www.i10.org.uk/node/51

Social Enterprise Training and Support
www.setas.co.uk

Forth Sector
Free resources including a comprehensive business planning guide.
www.forthsector.org.uk

Free basic business plans
www.bplans.com

Beermat Entrepreneur
www.beermat.biz

Marketing Judo
www.marketingjudo.co.uk

Legal structures for social enterprise (UK)
www.businesslink.gov.uk/socialenterprise

Support and funding

UK & Europe

Schwab Foundation
Network of outstanding individual social entrepreneurs throughout the world linked
to the World Economic Forum, based in Switzerland. www.schwabfound.org

UnLtd
Provides a complete package of funding and support including an online community
to help would-be social entrepreneurs make their ideas a reality. Also produces No
Limits online magazine. www.unltd.org.uk

Social Enterprise Coalition
Offers resources and case studies. Separate networks for each region of the UK.
www.socialenterprise.org.uk

Business in the Community
Network of UK companies committed to social responsibility; many donate profes-
sional services under the ProHelp scheme. Also involved in the Global Partner
Network to extend the principle worldwide. www.bitc.org.uk/prohelp

US

Ashoka
Has representatives in dozens of countries in every major region. Publishes *Changemakers*, an online journal on social entrepreneurship around the world. www.ashoka.org

Skoll Foundation
Manages the Skoll Awards for Social Entrepreneurship. Runs an interactive forum, Social Edge. Made a documentary series showcasing the work of 12 social entrepreneurs in eight countries. www.skollfoundation.org

Echoing Green
US-based international fellowship of social entrepreneurs. www.echoinggreen.org

Social Fusion
Incubates, supports, funds and brokers relationships with social entrepreneurs. www.socialfusion.org

Institute for Social Entrepreneurs
Provides seminars, workshops and consulting services for social entrepreneurs in the US and elsewhere. www.socialent.org

Australia

Social Ventures Australia
Provides research and brokerage to match social investors with projects. www.socialventures.com.au

Australasian Social Entrepreneur Network
Membership network of social entrepreneurs in Australia and New Zealand. www.sen.org.au

Asia

Beijing Social Enterprise Research Group
Aims to promote the development of social economy and social enterprise in China. Connected to the Global Links Initiative. See www.glinet.org

Entrepreneurial Training for Innovative Communities
Training and development for social entrepreneurs in Japan. www.etic.or.jp

Singapore Innovation Park
An incubation centre and training service for social entrepreneurs. www.socialinnovationpark.org

Youth Social Enterprise Initiative
Supports youth social entrepreneurs in South and Southeast Asia, offering finance, training, networking and mentoring. www.ysei.org

Magazines, journals and newsletters

Social Enterprise Magazine
UK weekly with articles on social enterprise and regeneration.
www.socialenterprisemag.co.uk

Stanford Social Innovation Review
Quarterly online journal. www.ssireview.org

Online magazines, journals and newsletters are also produced by UnLtd, Ashoka and Skoll.

Videos and films

Muhammad Yunus talking: www.muhammadyunus.org/content/view/48/

PBS Frontline/WORLD online series on social entrepreneurs:
www.pbs.org/frontlineworld/stories/socialentrepreneurs.html

Also see Ashoka, Skoll and Schwab Foundation websites for films and clips.

Networks / communities

i-genius
A world community of social entrepreneurs that seeks to inspire a new generation of social business, social enterprise and social ventures. www.i-genius.org

Social Edge
Online interactive debates and resources from the Skoll Foundation
www.socialedge.org

UnLtd World
An online forum to encourage networking and sharing of best practice between social entrepreneurs. www.unltdworld.com

Nearbuyou
Local purchasing from social enterprises in the UK. www.nearbuyou.co.uk

Incubation / start-up

Everything you need to know about starting up and running your own business.
www.startups.co.uk

Serviced offices for the social sector in London www.can-online.org.uk

Creative networking space for social innovators in various cities across the world.
www.the-hub.net

Singapore Social Innovation Park; offers incubation for social entrepreneurs.
www.socialinnovationpark.org

Citylife's Cambridge Community Innovation Centre provides low-cost office and
workshop space to encourage new and expanding social enterprises.
www.citylifeltd.org

Websites

www.ted.com
Ideas worth spreading: inspiring talks by great thinkers and doers.

www.worldchanging.com
Hundreds of ideas for making a better world, especially relating to the environment.

www.wearewhatwedo.org
An initiative to encourage mass adoption of small behavioural changes that will
contribute to a better world.

www.pbs.org/now/enterprisingideas
US Public Broadcasting Service platform providing videos and discussions of social
entrepreneurs' work, sponsored by the Skoll Foundation.

www.unltdideasbank.org.uk www.globalideasbank.org
Forums for posting or picking up possible social innovation ideas.

Online personality tests

Gallup Strengthsfinder
Detailed analysis and practical advice not specific to entrepreneurship.
www.strengthsfinder.com

Belbin Team Roles
Useful when building a team. www.belbin.com
Brief summaries available free.
www.changingminds.org/explanations/preferences/belbin

Myers Briggs Personality Indicator
Official test for a fee. www.cpp.com
Free reduced version. www.humanmetrics.com.

PS You can visit the website for this book at **www.social-entrepreneur.org.uk** for more information, links and updates, and to give feedback.

Notes

1. Introduction

1. Gordon Brown, *Britain's Everyday Heroes*, Mainstream Publishing, 2007, pp. 10–11.
2. Speech at Coin Street Community Builders, January 2006.
3. For example, Alex Nicholls (ed.), *Social Entrepreneurship: New Models of Sustainable Social Change*, Oxford University Press, 2006 and Johanna Mair, Jeffrey Robinson and Kai Hockerts, *Social Entrepreneurship*, Palgrave Macmillan, 2006.
4. Charles Leadbeater, 'Whatever happened to the heroes?' *Social Enterprise Magazine*, April 2007.
5. Rebecca Harding, *Social Entrepreneurship Monitor*, London Business School, 2006.

2. What is a social entrepreneur?

1. Survey for Social Enterprise Day, November 2006, Cabinet Office.
2. David McClelland's classic *The Achieving Society*, Van Nostrand, 1961 is still highly regarded.
3. Anita Roddick, *Business as Unusual*, Thorsons, 2000, pp. 38–40.
4. Bill Bolton and John Thompson, *The Entrepreneur in Focus: Achieve your potential*, Thomson, 2003, p. 49.
5. Bolton and Thompson, *The Entrepreneur in Focus*, p. 63.
6. Bill Bolton and John Thompson, *Entrepreneurs: Talent, temperament and technique*, Butterworth Heinemann, 2000.
7. Bolton and Thompson, *The Entrepreneur in Focus*, p. 235.
8. Bolton and Thompson, *Entrepreneurs*, p. 3–4.
9. Rebecca Harding, *Social Entrepreneurship Monitor*, London Business School, 2006.
10. Charles Leadbeater, 'Whatever happened to the heroes?', *Social Enterprise Magazine*, April 2007.
11. Sergey Brin and Larry Page, www.investor.google.com/ipo_letter.html
12. Dawn Marshall, Christine Whitehead, Roland Lovatt and Rebecca Foreman, *Emmaus UK: Building on success*, Centre for Housing and Planning Research, Department of Land Economy, University of Cambridge, 2004.
13. Liam Black and Jeremy Nicholls, *There's No Business Like Social Business*, Cat's Pyjamas, 2004.
14. Sally Osberg and Roger Martin, 'Social entrepreneurship: The case for definition,' *Stanford Social Innovation Review*, Spring 2007.

15. Black and Nicholls, *There's No Business Like Social Business*, p.54.
16. Black and Nicholls, *There's No Business Like Social Business*, p.74.
17. Leadbeater, 'Whatever happened to the heroes?'
18. Anglia Polytechnic, *Working in Social Enterprise*, 2002.
19. Patrick Dixon, *Building a Better Business*, Profile Books, 2005.
20. Osberg and Martin, 'Social entrepreneurship.'
21. John Pearce, *Social Enterprise in Anytown*, Calouste Gulbenkian Foundation, 2003, especially the chapter by Alan Kay on social capital.

3. Could I be a social entrepreneur?

1. Duncan Bannatyne, *Anyone Can Do It*, Orion, 2006.
2. Bill Bolton and John Thompson, *Entrepreneurs: Talent, temperament and technique*, Butterworth Heinemann, 2000, especially pages 30–33.
3. For instance, Charlotte Chambers and Fiona Edwards-Stuart, 'Leadership in the social economy,' School for Social Entrepreneurship, London, 2007; the panel of respondents in Craig Dearden-Phillips, *Your Chance to Change the World: The no fibbing guide to social entrepreneurship*, Directory of Social Change, 2008; and characteristics shared by social entrepreneurs around the world identified in David Bornstein, *How to Change the World: Social entrepreneurs and the power of new ideas*, Oxford University Press, 2003.
4. Anne Miller, *The Myth of the Mousetrap: How to get your ideas adopted (and change the world)*, Cyan, 2007, p. 41 shows how even fundamental character themes can change with age and social or professional context, in some cases naturally and others intentionally.
5. As summarised by Bolton and Thompson, *Entrepreneurs*, p. 37.
6. Bolton and Thompson, *Entrepreneurs*, p. 38.
7. Bill Bolton and John Thompson, *The Entrepreneur in Focus: Achieve your potential*, Thomson, 2003, chapter 8.
8. The questions in each of the entrepreneurial sections are my own interpretation of Bolton and Thompson's published framework and do not imply their endorsement. The reader wanting a practical and easy-to-follow self-help guide is recommended to consult Bill Bolton and John Thompson, *The Entrepreneur in Focus: Achieve your potential*, Thomson, 2003; and for those with a more academic interest, their *Entrepreneurs: Talent, temperament and technique*, Butterworth Heinemann, 2nd edition, 2004.
9. Bill Drayton's criteria for Ashoka fellowship selection; see chapter 5 below.
10. Dearden-Phillips, *Your Chance to Change the World*, and Chambers and Edwards-Stuart, 'Leadership in the social economy.'
11. Bolton and Thompson, *The Entrepreneur in Focus*, p. 104.
12. Anne Miller's advice on how to get ideas adopted is touched on in chapter 8 but is well worth reading in full in *The Myth of the Mousetrap*.
13. Bolton and Thompson, *The Entrepreneur in Focus*, p. 113.
14. Bornstein, *How to Change the World*, chapter 18.
15. Bolton and Thompson, *The Entrepreneur in Focus*, p. 148.
16. Bolton and Thompson, *The Entrepreneur in Focus*, p. 79.
17. See the box in chapter 8.
18. Dearden-Phillips, *Your Chance to Change the World*, p. 17

19. Bolton and Thompson, *Entrepreneurs*, p. 17.
20. Bolton and Thompson, *The Entrepreneur in Focus*, p. 192.

4. Four leading social entrepreneurs

1. Muhammad Yunus and Alan Jolis, *Banker to the Poor*, Aurum, 1999. Other sources used in writing this case study were Muhammad Yunus, *Creating a World Without Poverty: Social business and the future of capitalism*, Public Affairs, New York, 2007; Skoll World Forum speeches 2004 and 2007; and www.grameen-info.org, www.muhammadyunus.org and www.ashoka.org.
2. Muhammad Yunus, 'Social business entrepreneurs are the solution' in Alex Nicholls (ed.), *Social Entrepreneurship: New models of sustainable social change*, Oxford University Press, 2006, p. 42.
3. Randeep Ramesh 'Banker to the world's poor wins Nobel peace prize,' *The Guardian*, 14 October 2006.
4. www.bigissue.com.
5. See his autobiography, *Some Luck*, Hamish Hamilton, 2002.
6. Vision 21, Evaluation of Big Issue, 2001.
7. Interview on www.MyBnk.org.
8. David Ewing Duncan, 'Biotech & creativity: Trying to save the world on a shoe-string budget,' *San Fransisco Chronicle*, 11 July 2004; Elizabeth Olson, 'In pursuit of the cure,' *New York Times*, 31 December 2006.
9. Zina Moukheiber, 'Protecting the orphan drugs,' Forbes.com, 12 September 2003.
10. Institute for OneWorld Health, www.oneworldhealth.org.
11. The African Summit on Roll Back Malaria, WHO/CDS/RBM/2000.17, World Health Organization, Geneva; also J. L. Gallup and J. D. Sachs, *The Economic Burden of Malaria*, Harvard Center for International Development, 1998.
12. www.artemisininproject.org.
13. Sally Osberg and Roger Martin, 'Social entrepreneurship: The case for definition,' *Stanford Social Innovation Review*, Spring 2007.
14. Tim Heffernan, *Esquire*, December 2005; other material for this case study drawn from Victoria Hale's profiles at the Schwab Foundation and Skoll Foundation.
15. Interview with Mike Nowak, Social Fusion www.socialfusion.org
16. Indigenous Stock Exchange (ISX) feature and profile at www.isx.org.au.
17. Interview with Mike Nowak.
18. Nick Mathiason, 'The colour of money just got greener,' *The Observer*, 13 April 2008.
19. *The End of Charity: Time for social enterprise*, Allen & Unwin, 2008.

5. Mega social entrepreneurs

1. Caroline Hsu, 'Entrepreneur for social change,' *US News*, 31 October 2005.
2. In 'A conversation with David Bornstein' at www.csrwire.com.
3. David Bornstein, *How to Change the World: Social entrepreneurs and the power of new ideas*, Oxford University Press, 2003, p. 18.
4. Ashoka 2006 impact brochure at www.ashoka.org/impact
5. Hsu, 'Entrepreneur for social change.'
6. Bornstein, *How to Change the World*, chapter 20.
7. Bill Drayton, 'Nothing more powerful,' video at www.ashoka.com

8. Anya Kamenetz, 'Moving pictures,' *Fast Company*, September 2006.
9. A slogan from Jeff Skoll's film company, Participant Productions.
10. Charles Handy, *The New Philanthropists: The new generosity*, Heinemann, 2006, p. 182.
11. Skoll Foundation, www.skollfoundation.org.
12. Quoted in Sally Osberg, 'On the social edge,' *Philanthropy World*, volume 12, issue 3.
13. Participant Productions, www.participantproductions.com.
14. Skoll Centre for Social Entrepreneurship, www.sbs.ox.ac.uk/skoll.
15. Quoted in Stephen Gaghan, 'Jeff Skoll, the maker of take-action movies,' *Time* magazine, 30 April 2006.
16. Osberg, 'On the social edge.'
17. Pamela Hartigan report on 2002 World Economic Forum, www.schwabfound.org.
18. All quotes taken from videos on www.schwabfound.org.

6. Extraordinary ordinary people

1. Schwab Foundation, www.schwabfound.org; see also www.worldtoilet.org.
2. James Baderman and Justine Law, *Everyday Legends: the ordinary people changing our world*, WW Publishing, 2006, p.14.
3. www.belu.org.
4. 'Profits save the world,' *Sunday Times*, 10 December 2006.
5. Somsook Boonyabancha, 'Scaling up slums and squatter settlements upgrading,' CODI research paper, 2005; see also her profile at www. ashoka.org.
6. Tim Smit, 'Think bigger and better,' *The Guardian*, 31 January 2007.
7. Tim Smit, *Eden*, Bantam Press, 2001.
8. Interview with John Elkington, www.sustainability.co.uk.
9. Smit, 'Think bigger and better.'
10. Voice '07 social enterprise conference speech, Manchester, available at www.socialenterprise.org.uk.
11. www.edenproject.com.
12. James Baderman and Justine Law, *Everyday Legends: The ordinary people changing our world*, WW Publishing, 2006, p. 37.
13. www.greenpastureshousing.co.uk.
14. Baderman and Law, *Everyday Legends*, p. 82.
15. www.carbonneutralcompany.com.
16. Baderman and Law, *Everyday Legends*, p. 85.
17. www.green-works.co.uk.
18. Baderman and Law, *Everyday Legends*, p. 112.

7. Seven types of social entrepreneur

1. Muhammad Yunus, 'Social business entrepreneurs are the solution', in Alex Nicholls (ed.), *Social Entrepreneurship: New Models of Sustainable Social Change*, Oxford University Press, 2006, p. 40.
2. Muhammad Yunus, *Creating a World Without Poverty: Social business and the future of capitalism*, Public Affairs, New York, 2007, p. 38.

3. Yunus, *Creating a World Without Poverty*, p. 82.
4. Identified by Sally Osberg and Roger Martin, 'Social entrepreneurship: The case for definition,' *Stanford Social Innovation Review*, Spring 2007 .
5. Helen Haugh, 'New strategies for a sustainable society: The growing contribution of social entrepreneurship,' *Business Ethics Quarterly*, volume 17, p. 749.
6. Charles Leadbeater and Sue Goss, *Civic Entrepreneurship*, Demos 1998.
7. ECT announced in June 2008 that its recycling division was being sold to May Gurney plc for £3.4 million: the first commercial sale of a social enterprise. Services will continue as normal, although it remains to be seen whether the business model will change over time.
8. James Baderman and Justine Law, *Everyday Legends: The ordinary people changing our world*, WW Publishing, 2006, p. 60.
9. SustainAbility / Skoll Foundation, *Growing Opportunity: Entrepreneurial solutions to insoluble problems*, SustainAbility, 2007, p. 4.
10. Patrick Dixon, *Building a Better Business*, Profile Books, 2005, chapter 18.
11. Quoted by Mark Walton of Every Action Counts in *Social Enterprise Magazine*, May 2007; *Stern Review on the Economics of Climate Change*, Her Majesty's Treasury, 2007.
12. Charles Handy, 'The secrets of the new philanthropists,' *Social Enterprise Magazine*, July 2007.
13. www.thankubank.com.
14. Charles Handy, *The New Philanthropists: The new generosity*, William Heinemann, 2006, p. 59
15. Handy, *The New Philanthropists*, p. 91·
16. Handy, *The New Philanthropists*, p. 69.
17. *Colin and Justin on the Estate*, Channel 5, January 2007.
18. Liam Black and Jeremy Nicholls, *There's No Business Like Social Business*, Cat's Pyjamas, 2004, p.120.
19. Andrew Mawson, *The Social Entrepreneur: Making communities work*, Atlantic Books, 2008, p. 164.
20. Craig Dearden-Phillips, *Your Chance to Change the World: The no fibbing guide to social entrepreneurship*, Directory of Social Change, 2008.
21. David Bornstein, *How to Change the World: Social entrepreneurs and the power of new ideas*, Oxford University Press, 2003, chapter 18.
22. Bornstein, *How to Change the World*, p. 233.
23. Quoted in Baderman and Law, *Everyday Legends*.
24. Handy, *The New Philanthropists*, p. 183.
25. Charlotte Chambers and Fiona Edwards-Stuart, 'Leadership in the social economy,' School for Social Entrepreneurship, London, 2007, cited in Dearden-Phillips, *Your Chance to Change the World*.
26. Bornstein, *How to Change the World*, pp. 278–9.

8. Do it yourself: 1 The beermat social entrepreneur

1. Mike Southon and Chris West, *The Beermat Entrepreneur*, Pearson Prentice Hall, 2005.
2. School for Social Entrepreneurs presentation at Skoll Forum, cited by Barbara Phillips, 'They keep the world turning,' Social Enterprise Magazine, May 2007.

3. The ten steps outlined here are a synthesis drawn from a variety of business-plan outlines and my own experience.
4. James Baderman and Justine Law, *Everyday Legends: The ordinary people changing our world*, WW Publishing, 2006, pp. 28–31.
5. Interview with Massive Change project, June 2004, www.massivechange.com.
6. John Barnes and Richard Richardson, *Marketing Judo: Building your business using brains not budget*, Prentice Hall, 2002.
7. Nic Frances biography at www.coolnrg.com/downloads
8. Baderman and Law, *Everyday Legends*, p. 85.
9. Edward de Bono, *Serious Creativity*, HarperCollins, 1992.
10. Baderman and Law, *Everyday Legends*, p.43.
11. Anne Miller, *The Myth of the Mousetrap*, Cyan, 2007 – an invaluable book for both social entrepreneurs and aspiring inventors.
12. Craig Dearden-Phillips's *Your Chance to Change the World: The no fibbing guide to social entrepreneurship*, Directory of Social Change, 2008 is full of practical ideas.
13. Malcolm Gladwell, *The Tipping Point*, Abacus, 2001.

9. Do it yourself: 2 The career social entrepreneur

1. James Baderman and Justine Law, *Everyday Legends: The ordinary people changing our world*, WW Publishing, 2006, p. 26.
2. Interview on ISX (Indigenous Stock Exchange) at www.isx.org.au/people/frances_nic.
3. Alison Benjamin, 'Recipe for success,' *The Guardian*, 10 May 2006.
4. www.tiptheplanet.com.
5. www.brightgreentalent.com.
6. See www.primetimers.org.uk.
7. Jonathan Robinson and Carmel McConnell, *Careers Un-ltd*, Pearson Education, 2003. The book has the great subtitle: 'Tell me, what is it you plan to do with your one wild and precious life?'
8. See www.careershifters.org.
9. Rebecca Harding, *Social Entrepreneurship Monitor*, London Business School, 2006.
10. James Baderman and Justine Law, *Everyday Legends: the ordinary people changing our world*, WW Publishing, 2006.
11. www.youthbank.org.uk.
12. Michael Norton interview at www.MyBnk.org.
13. Their video footage is at www.cusec.org.uk.
14. Survey response in Craig Dearden-Phillips, *Your Chance to Change the World: The no fibbing guide to social entrepreneurship*, Directory of Social Change, 2008.
15. All figures from David Bornstein, *How to Change the World: Social entrepreneurs and the power of new ideas*, Oxford University Press, 2003, p.4.
16. Bornstein, *How to Change the World*, p.240.
17. Quoted in Alan Lodge, 'Drop in new UK business start-ups,' *Accountancy Magazine*, 24 June 2008. Some of these new businesses will be social enterprises, though no breakdown exists.
18. Tom Savage in Gordon Brown, *Britain's Everyday Heroes*, Mainstream Publishing, 2007, p. 201.

19. Bill Drayton interview with Massive Change project, June 2004, at www.massivechange.com.

10. The big issues: manifesto pledges for social entrepreneurs

1. SustainAbility / Skoll Foundation, *Growing Opportunity: Entrepreneurial solutions to insoluble problems*, SustainAbility, 2007.
2. United Nations, International Panel on Climate Change, November 2007.
3. Habitat for Humanity, www.habitat.org.
4. www.dreamscheme.net.
5. Richard Wilkinson, *The Impact of Inequality: How to make sick societies healthier*, Routledge, 2005.
6. Andrew Mawson, *The Social Entrepreneur: Making communities work*, Atlantic Books, 2008.
7. World Bank, *Global Monitoring Report*, 2007.
8. At the time of writing, Negroponte's initiative is locked in a battle with Intel, which withdrew from OLPC and launched its own low-cost laptop aimed at the developing world. As this suggests, large socially entrepreneurial initiatives can find themselves in a high-stakes commercial fight that they may not win – though as a determined social entrepreneur, Negroponte is fighting on.
9. C. K. Prahalad, *The Fortune at the Bottom of the Pyramid: Eradicating poverty through profits*, Wharton School Publishing, 2004.
10. Yunus, Muhammad, 'Social business entrepreneurs are the solution,' in Alex Nicholls (ed.), *Social Entrepreneurship: New Models of Sustainable Social Change*, Oxford University Press, 2006, p. 39.
11. www.muhammadyunus.org.
12. www.muhammadyunus.org.
13. Douglas McGray, 'Network philanthropy,' *LA Times*, 21 January 2007.
14. McGray, 'Network philanthropy.'
15. Schwab Foundation video.
16. See www.missionfish.org.
17. Speech to Social Entrepreneurs Network, Melbourne, Australia, April 2002 http://www.ideaas.org.br/midia/midia_schwab_melbourne_2002.htm.
18. Daniel Pink, *A Whole New Mind: Why right-brainers will rule the future*, Cyan, 2006.
19. Quoted in Deborah Tarrant, 'Champions of change,' *CPA Australia*, June 2007, volume 77, p. 44–7.
20. SustainAbility / Skoll Foundation, *Growing Opportunity: Entrepreneurial solutions to insoluble problems*, SustainAbility, 2007.
21. Charles Leadbeater, 'Whatever happened to the heroes?' *Social Enterprise Magazine*, April 2007.
22. Muhammad Yunus, *Creating a World Without Poverty: Social business and the future of capitalism*, Public Affairs, New York, 2007.
23. www.participate.net.
24. John Elkington and Pamela Hartigan, *The Power of Unreasonable People: How social entrepreneurs create markets that change the world*, Harvard Business School Press, 2008.
25. Tarrant, *CPA Australia*.

26. Emmanuel Faber, managing director of Danone Asia, quoted in Yunus, *Creating a World Without Poverty*, p. 161.
27. Anya Kamenetz, 'Moving Pictures,' *Fast Company* 108, September 2006.
28. Schwab Foundation video.
29. Yunus, *Creating a World Without Poverty*, p. 101.

11. A vision: transforming the personal and the planet

1. Barbara Phillips, 'They keep the world turning', *Social Enterprise Magazine*, May 2007.
2. New Economics Foundation evaluation of School for Social Entrepreneurs, October 2006.
3. Liam Black and Jeremy Nicholls, *There's No Business Like Social Business*, Cat's Pyjamas, 2004, p. 156.
4. Johanna Mair, Jeffrey Robinson and Kai Hockerts, *Social Entrepreneurship*, Palgrave Macmillan, 2006, p. 242.
5. John Elkington, 'Growing opportunity' news release, 28 March 2007, at www.sustainability.com.
6. Speech at Harvard University, 7 June 2007, www.gatesfoundation.org/media-center/speeches.
7. Social Edge discussion forum, 'What does it take to be a social entrepreneur?' September 2003, www.socialedge.org/discussions.
8. Paul Achleitner, chief financial officer, Allianz insurance, speaking at Skoll Forum 2007 reported in *Social Enterprise Magazine*, May 2007.
9. Bill Drayton interview with Massive Change project, June 2004, www.massivechange.com.
10. Pamela Hartigan, 'The challenge for social entrepreneurship', Schwab Foundation for Social Entrepreneurship Global Summit, Brazil, 2004.

About the author

Martin Clark is development director of Citylife, a national social investment charity based in Cambridge. After taking a first degree in geography, he set up a youth employment charity in Sheffield, lived and worked with unemployed people, and carried out research into unemployment for his PhD. His career as a social entrepreneur began twelve years ago when he helped set up a social enterprise promoting alternative financial products to help people invest in their own communities. In his spare time, he enjoys goalkeeping, driving an old camper van and spending the night on mountain tops.

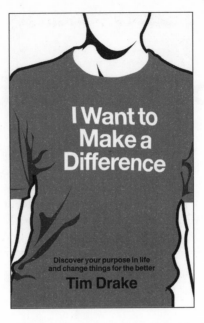

In the fast-moving world of today, how can an individual make a difference?

Most of us want to make a positive difference to the lives of our fellow human beings, but we're not entirely sure how to go about it. In *I Want to Make a Difference,* Tim Drake explains the Make a Difference Mindset, an action plan to make us more effective at making a difference in our chosen domain. It offers us a voyage with a clear goal at its end. The Mindset creates an unshakeable inner confidence so that each individual can change things for the better.

You too can be a Difference Driver, a Difference Deliverer, or a Beneficial Presence — or even all three, at different times and in different contexts. You can make life better for your family, your colleagues, your customers — and not least — for yourself.

In clear language and using well-drawn examples, Tim Drake explains how we can discover our purpose, and in doing so find fulfillment and ultimately bring meaning both to our lives and the lives of others.

ISBN 978-1-904879-63-3 / £9.99 Paperback

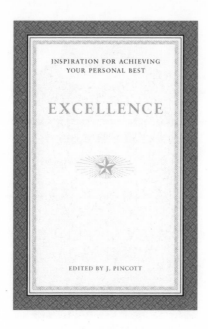

INSPIRATION FOR ACHIEVING
YOUR PERSONAL BEST

EXCELLENCE

EDITED BY J. PINCOTT

What uncommon quality do certain CEOs, rock stars, poets, architects, historians, politicians, and religious leaders have in common?

Excellence.

In every profession are people whose lives are distinguished by true excellence. Think of the Dalai Lama, Muhammad Yunus, Barack Obama, Steven Spielberg, Toni Morrison and Warren Buffett. How did they get to greatness?

This book is a collection of more than 300 quotes and passages on excellence from some of the world's most fascinating thinkers and leaders. Thematically organized as a handbook of little lessons, *Excellence* touches upon passion, creativity, discipline, ethics, flexibility, intuition, and incisiveness. Here is a guide for all who strive to achieve their personal best.

ISBN 978-1-904879-89-3 / £9.99 Hardback

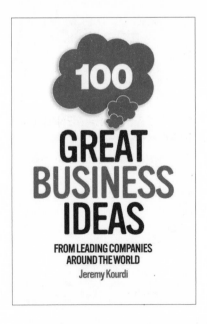

Know how to prepare a deep-dive prototype? How's your social networking? And are you up to speed in your psychographic profiling and vendor lock-in procedures?

In the world of business, new ideas and energy are needed constantly – in many ways and at varying times – to ensure success. This book contains 100 insightful and useful business ideas that will help you succeed.

Written in a stimulating and flexible way, *100 Great Business Ideas* contains ideas with proven power and potency that actually work. The ideas are varied, interesting, and thought-provoking, and some of the best ideas used in business. Some are simple – sometimes almost embarrassingly so – while others are based on detailed research and brilliant intellect.

If you have a restless desire and the energy to do well and stay ahead of the competition and a willingness to experiment and take a risk, this book will inspire you to find out more or develop your thinking along new, creative lines, generating brilliant ideas for the future.

ISBN 978-1-905736-07-X / £8.99 Paperback

Persuading people of our point of view and getting them to back our judgement with their money is what makes the business world go round. And the sharpest end of the persuasion business is the pitch: that intense and brief period when you get to make your case to the potential client. How you make the most of that opportunity is what this book is all about.

Why are so many people in so many companies so bad at pitching their services to potential clients? Why do so many companies come a "close second" when they pitch against their competitors? Why? Because pitching for business is the last bastion of amateurism in an otherwise wholly professionalized business economy.

There are hundreds of thousands of books written about how to motivate your staff, how to lead, how to operate more efficiently or how to transform an organization. And yet there is virtual silence on the single biggest issue facing all businesses: how to pitch and win clients. Without clients you don't have a business. Without clients you don't have anyone to motivate, you have no one to lead, you have nothing to operate or anything to transform. New business is the genesis of all other things.

Whether you're a sole trader or in charge of a multinational conglomerate, this book will turbo-charge your new business pitch performance. If you want to win more pitches for more clients and beat your competitors more often, *Pitching to Win* was written for you.

ISBN 978-1-905736-24-9 / £8.99 Paperback